Universal Basic Skills:

WHAT COUNTRIES STAND TO GAIN

Eric A. Hanushek
and Ludger Woessmann

Please cite this publication as:
OECD (2015), *Universal Basic Skills: What Countries Stand to Gain*, OECD Publishing.
http://dx.doi.org/10.1787/9789264234833-en

ISBN 978-92-64-23481-9 (print)
ISBN 978-92-64-23483-3 (PDF)

Photo credits:
© Istock.com/Riccardo Lennart Niels Mayer
© Istock.com/shironosov
© corbis_infinite - Fotolia.com
© Istock.com/Zurijeta
© freshidea - Fotolia.com

Corrigenda to OECD publications may be found on line at: *www.oecd.org/publishing/corrigenda*.

Foreword

Economic growth and social development are closely related to the skills of the population, indicating that a central post-2015 development goal for education should be that all youth achieve at least basic skills as a foundation for work and further learning, not merely that they gain access to schooling. Achieving such a goal would lead to remarkable overall economic gains while providing for broad participation in the benefits of development and facilitating poverty reduction, social and civic participation, health improvement, and gender equity.

To inform the post-2015 development agenda, this report provides the most comprehensive picture to date of the quality of learning outcomes around the world and then estimates the long-term economic gains of improving access to education and raising the quality of learning outcomes. The economic benefit of achieving universal basic skills has tremendous potential as a way to address issues of poverty and limited healthcare, and to foster the new technologies needed to improve the sustainability and inclusiveness of growth. No substitute for improved skills has been identified that offers similar possibilities of facilitating the inclusive growth needed to address the full range of development goals.

As the report shows, many countries could feasibly meet the goal of universal basic skills over the next decade and a half, assuming they duplicate the record of the most rapidly improving education systems.

The report was written by Eric Hanushek, Senior Fellow, Hoover Institution of Stanford University and Ludger Woessmann, Professor of Economics, University of Munich and Director, Ifo Center for the Economics of Education. The project was suggested by Andreas Schleicher, who provided valuable comments along the way. He and Qian Tang wrote the editorial. Christian Kastrop and other members of the OECD Economics Department provided helpful comments and suggestions; the PISA Governing Board also provided comments and advice. Juliet Evans provided an array of useful information about the PISA tests. The OECD provided the boxes on country improvements in PISA. Anne Himmelfarb provided exceptional editorial assistance. The production of the report was co-ordinated by Sophie Limoges and Marilyn Achiron. Support was provided by the Hoover Institution.

Table of contents

Editorial ... 9

Executive summary ... 15

Chapter 1 THE CASE FOR PROMOTING UNIVERSAL BASIC SKILLS... 19

Economic growth and sustainable social development ... 20

A new definition of literacy ... 21

Structure of the report ... 22

Chapter 2 RELATIONSHIP BETWEEN SKILLS AND ECONOMIC GROWTH ... 25

Chapter 3 THE GOAL: EVERY YOUNG PERSON ACQUIRES BASIC SKILLS ... 29

Chapter 4 DISTANCE FROM THE GOAL OF BASIC SKILLS FOR ALL... 35

Average achievement and lack of basic skills in participating countries ... 36

Achievement of other countries on regional tests ... 41

School enrolment in participating countries ... 43

The development challenge ... 44

Chapter 5 ECONOMIC IMPACTS OF ACHIEVING THE BASIC SKILLS GOAL BY 2030 ... 47

Projection model and parameter choices ... 48

Increasing average achievement of current students by 25 PISA points ... 49

Achieving gender equality in achievement among current students ... 51

Scenario I: Each current student attains a minimum of 420 PISA points ... 54

Scenario II: Achieving full participation in secondary school at current quality ... 58

Scenario III: Achieving full participation in secondary school and every student attains a minimum of 420 PISA points ... 61

Scenario IV: Scenario III with 30-year improvement ... 66

Robustness of projections ... 68

Summary of the economic impacts of educational improvement ... 71

Chapter 6 SHARING THE BENEFITS OF UNIVERSAL BASIC SKILLS ... 75
Variations in skills and in income ... 76
Basic skills for all and/or cultivating top achievers ... 77

Chapter 7 WHAT ACHIEVING UNIVERSAL BASIC SKILLS MEANS FOR THE ECONOMY AND FOR EDUCATION ... 81

Annexes

Annex A **REVIEW OF KNOWLEDGE CAPITAL AND GROWTH** ... 88

Annex B **TRANSFORMING PERFORMANCE IN TIMSS ONTO THE PISA SCALE** ... 95

Annex C **AUGMENTED NEOCLASSICAL RESULTS** ... 99

Annex D **DISTRIBUTION OF SKILLS WHEN GOAL OF UNIVERSAL BASIC SKILLS IS ACHIEVED** ... 102

Annex E **SAMPLE OF PISA QUESTIONS REQUIRING LEVEL 1 SKILLS** ... 103

Figures

Figure ES.1 Effect on GDP of achieving universal basic skills (in % of current GDP) 17

Figure 2.1 Knowledge capital and economic growth rates across countries 26

Figure 4.1 Average performance on international student achievement tests 37

Figure 4.2 Share of students not acquiring basic skills....38

Figure 4.3 Average performance of Latin American countries on international and regional student achievement tests 41

Figure 4.4 Average performance of sub-Saharan African countries on international and regional student achievement tests 42

Figure 4.5 Secondary school enrolment rates....44

Figure 5.1 Effect on GDP of every current student acquiring basic skills (in % of current GDP) 57

Figure 5.2 Effect on GDP of universal enrolment in secondary school at current school quality (in % of current GDP) 61

Figure 5.3 Effect on GDP of universal enrolment in secondary school and every student acquiring basic skills (in % of current GDP) 64

Figure 5.4 Effect on GDP of universal enrolment in secondary school and every student acquiring basic skills (in % of discounted future GDP) 65

Figure 5.5 How the impact of knowledge capital on growth varies by economic institutions 70

Figure 7.1 Annual improvement in student achievement, 1995-2009 83

Tables

Table ES.1 Gains from policy outcomes as percent of current GDP 17

Table 5.1 Effect on GDP of increasing average performance of current students by 25 PISA points 49

Table 5.2 Effect on GDP of attaining gender equality in achievement among current students 52

Table 5.3 Effect on GDP of every current student acquiring basic skills ..55

Table 5.4 Effect on GDP of universal enrolment in secondary school at current school quality 59

Table 5.5 Effect on GDP of universal enrolment in secondary school and every student acquiring basic skills 62

Table 5.6 Effect on GDP of universal enrolment in secondary school and every student acquiring basic skills, achieved over 30 years....66

Table 5.7 Comparison of estimates with endogenous and augmented neoclassical growth models 69

Table 5.8 Summary of gains from separate policy options 71

Table A.1 Basic growth regressions: Long-run growth in per capita GDP, 1960-2000 89

Table B.1 Country performance, enrolment rates, income and population 96

Table B.2 Performance of countries that lack internationally comparable GDP data 98

Table C.1 Lower-bound projection results from augmented neoclassical model specification 99

Table D.1 Means and standard deviations of performance, before and after attaining universal basic skills 102

Editorial

Education post-2015: Knowledge and skills transform lives and societies

by Andreas Schleicher, Director for Education and Skills, OECD
Qian Tang, Assistant Director-General, UNESCO

Everywhere, skills transform lives, generate prosperity and promote social inclusion. If there is one lesson we have learned from the global economy over the past few years, it is that we cannot simply bail ourselves out of an economic crisis, we cannot solely stimulate ourselves out of an economic crisis, and we cannot just print money to ease our way out of an economic crisis. We can only grow ourselves out of bad economic conditions and, in the long run, that depends more than anything on equipping more people with better skills to collaborate, compete and connect in ways that drive our societies forward – and on using those skills productively. Ensuring that all people have a solid foundation of knowledge and skills must therefore be the central aim of the post-2015 education agenda.

This is not primarily about providing more people with more years of schooling; in fact, that's only the first step. It is most critically about making sure that individuals acquire a solid foundation of knowledge in key disciplines, that they develop creative, critical thinking and collaborative skills, and that they build character attributes, such as mindfulness, curiosity, courage and resilience.

Every three years, some 70 countries compare how well their school systems prepare young people for life and work. The framework for these comparisons is the world's premier metric for learning outcomes, an international assessment of the knowledge and skills of 15-year-old students known as PISA, the Programme for International Student Assessment. PISA does not just examine whether students have learned what they were taught, but also assesses whether students can creatively and critically use what they know. Of course, such international comparisons are never easy and they aren't perfect. But they show what is possible in education and they help governments to see themselves in comparison to the education opportunities and results delivered by the world's education leaders.

Low performance in education carries a high cost

This report takes those comparisons a step further in the context of education post-2015. Looking at the historic relationship between improved skills and economic growth, the authors quantify the economic implications of improved schooling outcomes.

The first thing the results show is that the quality of schooling in a country is a powerful predictor of the wealth that countries will produce in the long run. Or, put the other way around, the economic output that is lost because of poor education policies and practices leaves many countries in what amounts to a permanent state of economic recession – and one that can be larger and deeper than the one that resulted from the financial crisis at the beginning of the millennium, out of which many countries are still struggling to climb.

Ensuring universal access to schooling at the current quality of education yields some economic gains, particularly in the lower-income countries. But improving the quality of schools so that every student reaches at least the baseline Level 1 of performance on the PISA scale – where students demonstrate elementary skills to read and understand simple texts and master basic mathematical and scientific concepts and procedures – has a much, much larger impact on the economy. The report shows that if every

15-year-old student in the world reached at least the baseline Level 1 of performance on the PISA scale by 2030 the benefits for economic growth and sustainable development would be enormous.

Among the countries compared, Ghana has the lowest enrolment rate in secondary schools (46%) and also the lowest achievement levels for those 15-year-olds who are in school (291 PISA points). While it is difficult for Ghana to meet the goal of universal basic skills any time soon, if it did, it would see a gain over the lifetime of its children born today that, in present value terms, is 38 times its current GDP. This is equivalent to tripling Ghana's discounted future GDP every four years during the working life of those students with improved skills.

For lower-middle income countries, the discounted present value of future gains would still be 13 times current GDP and would average out to a 28% higher GDP over the next 80 years. And for upper-middle income countries, which generally show higher levels of learning outcomes, it would average out to a 16% higher GDP.

High-quality schooling and oil don't mix easily

The goal of universal basic skills also has meaning for high-income countries, most notably the oil-producing countries. Many of them have succeeded in converting their natural capital into physical capital and consumption today; but they have failed to convert their natural capital into the human capital that can generate the economic and social outcomes to sustain their future. The report shows that the high-income non-OECD countries, as a group, would see an added economic value equivalent to almost five times the value of their current GDP – if they equipped all students with at least basic skills. So there is an important message for countries rich in natural resources: the wealth that lies hidden in the undeveloped skills of their populations is far greater than what they now reap by extracting wealth from natural resources. And there is more: PISA shows a significantly negative relationship between the money countries earn from their natural resources and the knowledge and skills of their school population. So PISA and oil don't mix easily. Exceptions such as Australia, Canada and Norway, which are rich in natural resources and still score reasonably well on PISA, have all established deliberate policies of saving these resource rents, not just consuming them.

One interpretation is that in countries with little in the way of natural resources – such as Finland, Japan and Singapore – education is highly valued, and produces strong outcomes, at least partly because the public at large has understood that the country must live by its knowledge and skills, and that these depend on the quality of education. In other words, the value that a country places on education may depend, at least in part, on a country's view of how knowledge and skills fit into the way it makes its living.

High income doesn't protect against shortcomings in education

One might be tempted to think that high-income countries have had all the means to eliminate extreme underperformance in education and should already have achieved the post-2015 education goal and targets. But the report shows otherwise. For example, 24% of 15-year-olds in the United States do not successfully complete even the basic Level 1 PISA tasks. If the United States were to ensure that all students meet the goal of universal basic skills, the economic gains could reach over USD 27 trillion in additional income for the American economy over the working life of these students.

So even high-income OECD countries would gain significantly from bringing all students up to basic skills by 2030. For this group of countries, average future GDP would be 3.5% higher than it would be otherwise. That is close to what these countries currently spend on their schools. In other words, the economic gains that would accrue solely from eliminating extreme underperformance in high-income OECD countries by 2030 would be sufficient to pay for the primary and secondary education of all students.

Such improvements are entirely realistic in the timescale of the post-2015 education agenda. For example, Poland was able to reduce the share of underperforming students by one-third, from 22% to 14%, within less than a decade. Shanghai in China reduced the share of underperforming students between 2009 and 2012 alone from 4.9% to 3.8%.

And, of course, more ambitious improvements can have much larger potential gains. The calculations involving the movement of all students to basic skills are lower-bound estimates because they assume that the improvement in schools does not affect anybody with higher skills. However, evidence from PISA indicates that school reforms that lead to improved performance at the lower end of the distribution invariably also help those higher in the distribution.

Achieving basic skills would make economic growth more inclusive

A great strength of the universal basic skills objectives for the post-2015 education agenda highlighted in this report is the contribution it would make to inclusive growth. As the authors show, achieving the development goal of universal basic skills has a complementary impact on reducing gaps in earnings that filter into smaller income differences. And it has this impact while also expanding the size of the economy. In this sense, it differs from simple tax and redistribution schemes that might change the income distribution but do not add to societal output. Thus, more inclusive growth made possible through universal achievement of basic skills has tremendous potential to ensure that the benefits of economic development are shared more equitably among citizens. No substitute for improved skills has been identified that offers similar possibilities of facilitating the inclusive growth needed to address the full range of the 17 post-2015 sustainable development goals (SDGs).

While the data show clearly how poor skills severely limit people's access to better-paying and more rewarding jobs, results from the 2012 Survey of Adult Skills also show that individuals with poorer foundation skills are far more likely than those with advanced literacy skills to report poor health, to believe that they have little impact on political processes, and not to participate in associative or volunteer activities.

Excellence and equity are compatible policy targets in the post-2015 education agenda

As important as the achievement of universal basic skills is, the well-being of nations also depends critically on the share of high-skilled workers in the talent pool. The authors show that the economic impact of the share of students with basic skills is similar across all levels of development. However, the economic impact of the top-performing share of students is significantly larger in countries that have more scope to catch up to the most productive countries, and the process of economic convergence seems accelerated in countries with larger shares of high-performing students. This underlines the importance, particularly for middle-income countries, of investing in excellence in education.

Interestingly, the interaction between the top-performing and basic-literacy shares of students in the authors' growth models appears to produce a complementarity between basic skills and top-level skills: in order to be able to implement the imitation and innovation strategies developed by the most-skilled workers, countries need a workforce with at least basic skills. Investments in excellence and equity in education thus seem to reinforce each other. When countries develop a student population with strong foundation skills, they will be most likely to also develop a larger share of high performers.

There are some caveats to consider

Some may wonder how reliable such long-term projections can be in a post-2015 world that is increasingly complex, uncertain and volatile. However, the analyses in this report rely on just two major assumptions.

The first is that a better-educated workforce leads to a larger stream of new ideas that continues to produce technological progress at a higher rate. For some, that assumption may even seem conservative, given that the world is becoming increasingly knowledge-intensive and is rewarding better skills at an ever higher rate. For those who remain sceptical, the report provides an alternative scenario in which productivity is frozen, and every new worker will simply expand the pool of existing workers with similar skills and continue to work with the same productivity until the end of their working life. This rather pessimistic scenario, in which people just keep doing what they have been doing, leads to smaller but still impressive economic rewards for improved schooling.

The second assumption is that the improved skills will actually be used in the economy. Here, the Survey of Adult Skills shows that there are significant differences in how well different countries extract value from their talent. Indeed, the toxic coexistence of high unemployment and skill shortages in many countries underlines that point. The survey also shows that even the best skills can atrophy if they are not used effectively. So while improved schooling is a necessary condition for economic progress, countries also need to work on the quality of their institutions to ensure that they add higher value-added jobs to a labour market that helps to get more people with better skills working – and for better pay.

For example, governments need to provide the right institutions, incentives and tax policies to help the economy develop and labour markets work efficiently, to help people invest in their skills and get to the right place for the right job, and to link support to participation in activities that improve individuals' employability. Employers, too, can contribute by investing in learning and by offering adequate flexibility in the workplace. Labour unions need to balance employment protection for established and new workers, and help to ensure that investments in training are reflected in better-quality jobs and higher salaries. The authors factor these issues into the analyses by assuming that new skills in a country will be absorbed as effectively, on average, as has occurred across countries that had undergone similar transitions in their past. The report also examines how changes in the quality of social institutions can affect the economic impact of universal basic skills.

Last but not least, the report limits itself to examining the economic impact of mathematics and science knowledge and skills, simply because those can be measured reliably and consistently across countries and cultures. That leaves out important other skills and therefore suggests that the economic impact of skills in this report is underestimated. It also highlights that the post-2030 world will need to work on broadening the measurement of skills to encompass a wider range of cognitive, social and emotional dimensions that are relevant to the future of individuals and societies. This is already a major priority for PISA.

Yes, we can achieve improved learning outcomes by 2030

The message of these rather complex analyses is simple: there is no shortcut to improved learning outcomes in a post-2015 world economy where knowledge and skills have become the global currency, the key to better jobs and better lives. And there is no central bank that prints this currency. We cannot inherit this currency, and we cannot produce it through speculation; we can only develop it through sustained effort and investment in people. That raises the question of whether the improvements in learning outcomes suggested in this report are realistic – and how they can be achieved by 2030.

The answer to the first question is unambiguously positive. PISA shows that top performers in education, such as Shanghai in China, Korea and Singapore, were able to further extend their lead over the past years, and countries like Brazil, Mexico, Tunisia and Turkey achieved major improvements from previously low levels of performance – all at a speed that exceeds, by a large margin, the improvements described in this report. The example of Brazil is particularly significant, as the country was able to substantially raise both participation and outcomes over the past decade.

Even those who claim that the performance of students mainly reflects social and cultural factors must therefore concede that improvements in education are possible. A culture of education isn't just inherited, it is created by what we do. Of the 13 OECD countries that significantly improved their learning outcomes as measured by PISA between 2003 and 2012, three also show improvements in equity in education during the same period, and another nine improved their performance while maintaining an already high level of equity – proving that countries do not have to sacrifice high performance to achieve equity in education opportunities. For example, Germany was able to significantly raise learning outcomes and close socio-economic gaps by half; and a major overhaul of Poland's school system helped to dramatically reduce performance variations among schools and improve overall performance by more than half a school year.

No, it's not just about money

The answer to the second question remains the subject of extensive research and analysis. Clearly, there are wide differences between countries in the quality of learning outcomes. The equivalent of almost six years of schooling separate the highest and lowest average performances of the countries that took part in the latest PISA mathematics assessment.

But there is now also considerable knowledge about the policies and practices that relate to improved learning. The individual, school-level and systemic factors that have been measured by PISA alone explain 85% of the performance variation among schools in the participating countries, so we know that improved schooling outcomes do not come about haphazardly.

Resources are part of the answer. In particular, for countries that currently invest less than USD 50 000 per student between the age of 6 and 15, the data show an important relationship between spending per student and the quality of learning outcomes. But money alone gets education systems just up to a point. In fact, among the countries that invest at least USD 50 000 per student between the age of 6 and 15 – and they include all high-income and many middle-income countries – the data no longer show a relationship between spending and the quality of learning outcomes. In other words, two countries with similarly high spending levels can produce very, very different results. So for the countries that have ensured an essential level of funding, it is not primarily about how much they spend on education, but about how they spend their resources. For example, whenever high-performing education systems have to make a choice between a smaller class and a better teacher, they go for the latter.

So there is a striking asymmetry in the relationship between skills and money. While improved skills consistently generate more money for individuals and nations, improved skills do not automatically require more money. As a result, the world is no longer divided neatly into rich and well-educated countries and poor and badly educated ones. With the right policies, countries can break out of the cycle of poor outcomes in education leading to poor economic outcomes in the timescale envisaged in the post-2015 education agenda.

Underperformance is also not just an issue of poor kids from poor neighbourhoods; it is an issue for many kids in many neighbourhoods and many countries. The large share of students from advantaged backgrounds, in some of the wealthiest countries, who do not attain even basic skills proficiency is worrying. And the fact that the 10% most disadvantaged children in Shanghai outperform the 10% most advantaged children in large parts of Europe and the United States reminds us that poverty isn't destiny. No one can afford to be complacent.

All of this shows that improvements in learning outcomes can be achieved by all countries by 2030 with the right education policies and practices.

We can learn from good examples

So what can we learn from the world's education leaders? The first lesson from PISA is that the leaders in high-performing school systems seem to have convinced their citizens to make choices that value education more than other things. Chinese parents and grandparents tend to invest their last renminbi into the education of their children, their future. In much of Europe and North America, governments have started to borrow the money of their children to finance their consumption today and the debt they have incurred puts a massive break on economic and social progress.

But placing a high value on education is just part of the equation. Another part is the belief in the success of every child. Top school systems expect every child to achieve and accept no excuse for failure. They realise that ordinary students have extraordinary talents and they embrace diversity with differentiated instructional practices.

And nowhere does the quality of a school system exceed the quality of its teachers. Top school systems pay attention to how they select and train their staff. They attract the right talent and they watch how they improve the performance of teachers who are struggling. They also provide intelligent pathways for teachers to grow in their careers.

High performers have also moved on from industrial to professional forms of work organisation in their schools. They encourage their teachers to use innovative pedagogies, to improve their own performance and that of their colleagues, and to work together to define good practice. They grow and distribute leadership throughout the school system. The goal of the past was standardisation and compliance; today's best school leaders enable their schools to be inventive.

Perhaps the most impressive outcome of world-class school systems is that they deliver high quality across the entire school system so that every student benefits from excellent teaching. School systems as diverse as those in Finland and Shanghai attract the strongest principals to the toughest schools and the most talented teachers to the most challenging classrooms.

Effective policies are usually far more easily designed than implemented. But the world provides plenty of examples of improvements in education, and there is no time to lose if we are to achieve the goal and targets set out in the post-2015 education agenda. Without the right skills, people end up on the margins of the society, technological progress doesn't translate into economic growth, and countries face an uphill struggle to remain ahead in this hyper-connected world. Ultimately in this scenario, the social glue that holds our societies together will disintegrate. The world has become indifferent to past reputations and unforgiving of frailty. Success will go to those individuals, institutions and countries that are swift to adapt, slow to complain and open to change. The task for governments is to help their citizens rise to this challenge by ensuring that by 2030 all of their people are equipped with the knowledge and skills they need for further education, work and life.

Executive summary

Discussions about expanding the Millennium Development Goals beyond 2015 acknowledge, in part, that the original goal of universal primary schooling should include a stronger component on learning outcomes. A focus on learning and skills is strongly supported by evidence about the economic benefits that accompany improved school quality. Economic growth and social development are closely related to the skills of a population, indicating that a central post-2015 development goal for education should be that all youth achieve at least basic skills as a foundation for work and further learning, not merely that they gain access to schooling. Achieving such a goal would lead to remarkable overall economic gains while providing for broad participation in the benefits of development.

Past policies that focus on education as the means of putting nations on the path of growth and development have met with mixed success. While they have substantially expanded worldwide access to schooling, in many countries they have not secured the hoped-for improvements in economic well-being. The simple explanation for this is that these policies did not sufficiently emphasise or appreciate the importance of learning outcomes or cognitive skills. History shows that it is these skills that drive economic growth. But these skills are not measured by simple school attainment; and access to schools, alone, turns out to be an incomplete and ineffective goal for development.

Measuring basic skills

This report measures skills based on the achievement of youth on international assessments of learning outcomes. Using data from 76 countries, it focuses on the portion of the population that lacks the basic skills needed for full participation in today's global economy. A straightforward and useful definition of basic skills is the acquisition of at least Level 1 skills (420 points) on the OECD Programme for International Student Assessment (PISA). This level of skills corresponds to what might today be called modern functional literacy.

Based on that framework, a clear and measurable development goal is that *all youth acquire basic skills*. This goal, which directly promotes inclusive development, incorporates two components: full enrolment of youth in secondary school, and sufficient achievement for economic and social participation. By measuring progress on a consistent basis across countries, this goal can be used to direct attention and resources toward long-run economic development.

Earlier research shows the causal relationship between a nation's skills – its knowledge capital – and its long-run growth rate, making it possible to estimate how education policies affect each nation's expected economic performance. The changes needed in order to reach universal achievement of basic skills can be assessed for each of the 76 countries that currently have data on school enrolment and on achievement, and the economic impact can be estimated directly from the historical achievement-growth relationship.

The economic returns to universal basic skills

This analysis incorporates the dynamics of education reform policies and their impact on the skills of each country's workforce. Changes in the workforce are based on school reforms that lead to achieving universal basic skills over a 15-year period ending in 2030. Over time, the knowledge capital of the nation improves as better-educated youth enter the labour force. The more skilled workforce leads to increased economic growth and other positive social outcomes. The economic value of the policy change is calculated as the difference between the GDP expected with the current workforce and the GDP expected with the improved workforce, calculated over the expected lifetime of a child born today.

As seen in Figure ES.1, which shows the projected economic gains as a percent of current GDP, the results would be stunning for all countries – even high-income OECD countries. While most of this latter group of countries have achieved nearly universal access to secondary schools, all continue to have a portion of their population that fails to achieve basic skills. On average, these countries would see a 3.5% higher discounted average GDP over the next 80 years – which is almost exactly the average percentage of GDP they devote to public primary and secondary school expenditure. These economic gains from solely eliminating extreme underperformance in high-income OECD countries would be sufficient to pay for all schooling.

In the lowest-income countries considered here, where the enrolment rate averages just 75%, the gains summarised in Table ES.1 from improving the current quality of schools are three times as large as those from expanding enrolment at the current quality. Across the middle income countries, the economic gains from achieving universal basic skills would average more than eight times their current GDP.

Universal basic skills and inclusive development

A great strength of the universal basic skills goal is the contribution it would make to inclusive growth. The goal would ensure that a wide variety of countries participate in – and benefit from – enhanced economic well-being. Within each country, the variation in earnings currently observed would shrink, and many more individuals would be able to engage productively in the labour market. The evidence of improvements in achievement over the past 15 years shows that many countries could meet the goal of universal basic skills over the next 15 years, assuming they duplicate the record of the best performers. But improvement is clearly difficult, and some countries have even seen their achievement levels fall. If countries wish to improve, there is no substitute for measuring achievement outcomes and evaluating policies on the basis of achievement.

The inclusive growth made possible through universal achievement of basic skills has tremendous potential as a way to address issues of poverty and limited health care, and to foster the new technologies needed to improve the sustainability of growth. No substitute for improved skills has yet been identified that offers similar possibilities of facilitating the inclusive growth needed to address the full range of development goals.

FIGURE ES.1 EFFECT ON GDP OF ACHIEVING UNIVERSAL BASIC SKILLS (in % of current GDP)

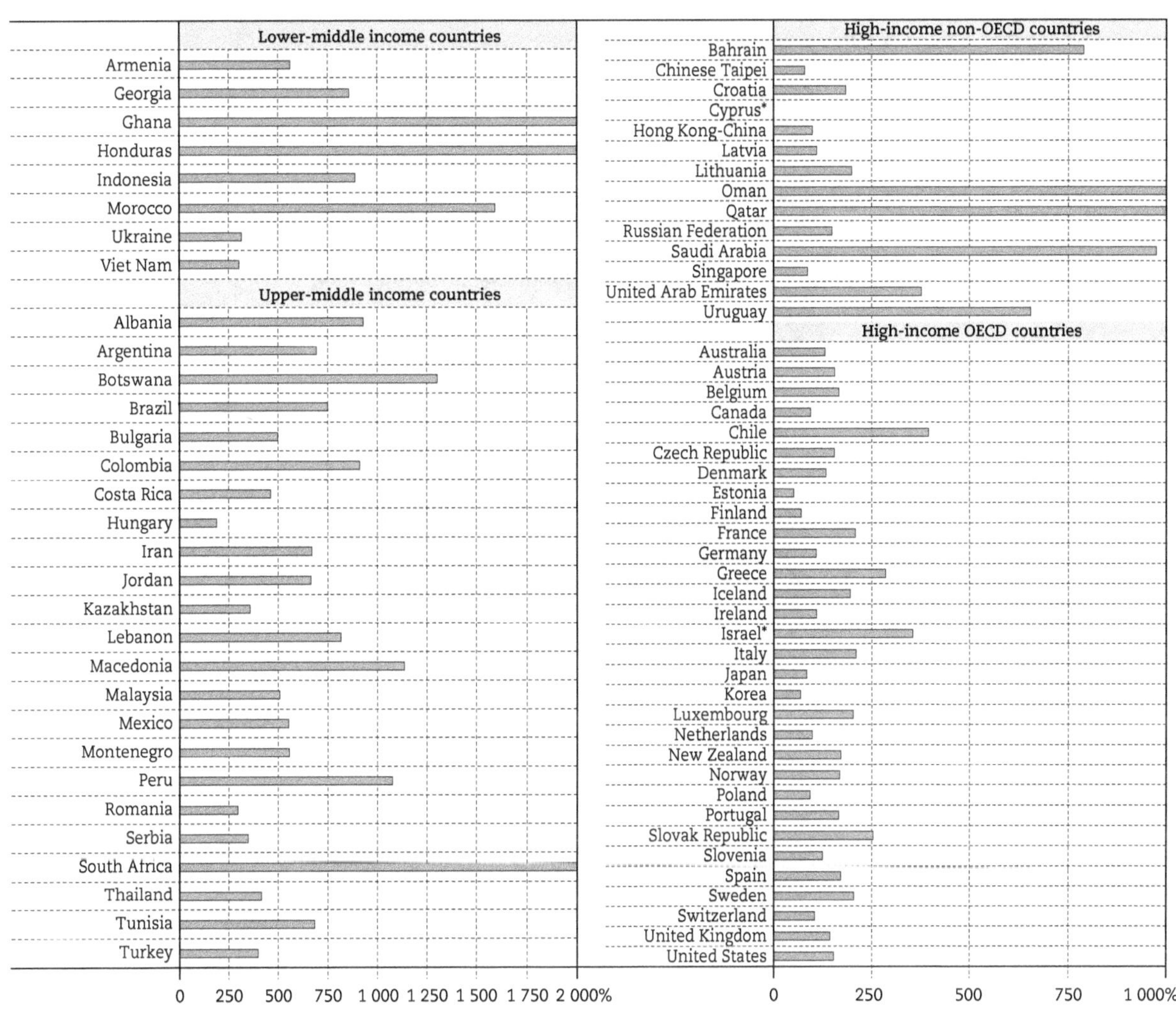

* See notes at the end of this summary.

Notes: Discounted value of future increases in GDP until 2095 due to a reform that achieves full participation in secondary school and brings each student at least to minimum of 420 PISA points, expressed as a percentage of current GDP. Value is 3 881% for Ghana, 2 016% for Honduras, 2 624% for South Africa, 1 427% for Oman and 1 029% for Qatar. See Table 5.5 for details.

TABLE ES.1 GAINS FROM POLICY OUTCOMES AS % OF CURRENT GDP

	Scenario I All current students to basic skills	Scenario II: Full enrollment at current quality	Scenario III: Universal basic skills
Lower-middle income countries	627%	206%	1 302%
Upper-middle income countries	480%	134%	731%
High-income non-OECD countries	362%	60%	473%
High-income OECD countries	142%	19%	162%

Notes: See Tables 5.3-5.5 for details.

Notes regarding Cyprus

Readers should note the following information provided by Turkey and by the European Union Member States of the OECD and the European Union regarding the status of Cyprus:

Note by Turkey

The information in this document with reference to "Cyprus" relates to the southern part of the Island. There is no single authority representing both Turkish and Greek Cypriot people on the Island. Turkey recognises the Turkish Republic of Northern Cyprus (TRNC). Until a lasting and equitable solution is found within the context of the United Nations, Turkey shall preserve its position concerning the "Cyprus issue".

Note by all the European Union member States of the OECD and the European Union

The Republic of Cyprus is recognised by all members of the United Nations with the exception of Turkey. The information in this document relates to the area under the effective control of the Government of the Republic of Cyprus.

Note regarding Israel

The statistical data for Israel are supplied by and under the responsibility of the relevant Israeli authorities. The use of such data by the OECD is without prejudice to the status of the Golan Heights, East Jerusalem and Israeli settlements in the West Bank under the terms of international law.

Chapter 1

The case for promoting universal basic skills

The key to achieving inclusive and sustainable development lies in increasing the knowledge and skills of populations. This chapter discusses the link between economic growth and a population's skills. It argues that all countries, rich and poor, stand to gain enormously by ensuring that all of their citizens acquire at least basic skills in reading, mathematics and science.

There is broad interest in extending and amplifying the Millennium Development Goals, and specifically in focusing on inclusiveness and sustainability of development. Success over the next decades, however, will ultimately depend on economic growth, which will expand economic opportunities and permit societies to achieve improved levels of well-being. This report puts the development goals into the context of history, which has shown that growth is directly related to the knowledge capital, or skills, of a country's population.[1] It underlines the importance that all youth achieve at least basic skills and not merely gain access to schooling.[2] Framing the measurement of education progress directly in terms of knowledge capital – the underlying force behind economic growth – makes it more likely that other broad development goals will be met.

Inclusive development rightly seeks broader participation by countries in world economic well-being and by individuals in their country's economic gains. Historically, the benefits of enhanced economic outcomes have not been equally shared across society. Even in the richest countries, a segment of the population has been left behind to deal with limited resources and limited opportunities. This segment has faced health insecurity, constrained job possibilities, and a myriad of other threats associated with poverty. The difficulties for this group are compounded when countries, as a whole, lag behind world improvement in economic outcomes.

Sustainable development calls for recognising the full cost of development. In the past, growth and development have come at the expense of the environment. These costs accumulate over time, leading to excessive pressures on the ecosystem that threaten the future. Sustainable development will depend on innovation that permits growth while preserving natural resources.

Economic growth and sustainable social development

This analysis concentrates on economic growth for the simple reason that growth expands the possibilities for both economic and social outcomes. It is often difficult to realise the importance of differences in growth rates, in particular because of the importance of compound interest when accrued over a long period of time. In fact, if per capita income grows at 4% for half a century, as in many East Asian countries, people are, on average, more than seven times as prosperous as less than two generations ago. If, instead, the growth rate is below 2%, as in Latin America, people are only about two-and-a-half times as prosperous as at the beginning of the period. And if the growth rate is 1%, as in many countries in sub-Saharan Africa, people are only one-and-a-half times as prosperous.

The key to achieving inclusive and sustainable development lies in increasing the knowledge and skills of populations. Knowledge-led growth, the hallmark of prosperity for the past half century, provides a path that converges on the overall goals of the broader world community.[3] Inclusive development is best pursued through expanded economic opportunities. Simply put, it is much easier to ensure inclusion and alleviate the burdens of poverty when the whole economic pie is larger. Expanded skills allow a broader segment of society to contribute to the economy; and this increased participation directly contributes to enhanced productivity and reduces the redistributive needs. (Within a fixed economy, even attempting to redistribute resources is generally politically difficult, and excessive redistribution may threaten the overall performance of the economy.) Expanded skills also facilitate sustainable development and growth because they lead to innovative capacity that allows economic advancement without simultaneously depleting environmental resources.

The issue of assuring basic skills for all is most acute in the development context, and this report therefore focuses attention there. To be sure, developing the skills of all members of society is a worthy objective and would lead to economic and social gains for both individuals and society. But, while the report addresses issues of focusing on the most advanced skills (see Chapter 6), it is most concerned with ensuring that all of society participates in the gains of development. This inclusiveness is more direct and feasible when all have the necessary skills for productive participation in the labour market.

A new definition of literacy

Without the necessary cognitive skills to compete and thrive in the modern world economy, many people are unable to contribute to and participate in development gains. Literacy was once defined in terms of the ability to read simple words. But in today's interconnected societies, it is far more. It is the capacity to understand, use and reflect critically on written information, the capacity to reason mathematically and use mathematical concepts, procedures and tools to explain and predict situations, and the capacity to think scientifically and to draw evidence-based conclusions.

Today, much of the world's population is functionally illiterate. The functional illiterates do not have the skills that employers seek and that the formal labour market rewards. If development occurs, citizens around the world will need the basic skills currently required in developed countries.

Because "functional literacy" has been given many meanings, the term is not used in this report. Instead, in exploring how countries could increase their knowledge capital and the implications of that increase, the analysis relies on a quantitative definition of "basic skills". In today's interconnected world, the required basic skills are not just being able to identify information and carry out routine procedures according to direct instructions. They also include such skills as locating needed information and making basic inferences of various types.[4]

In its policy paper on post-2015 education goals, UNESCO focuses directly on how the demand for skills has evolved:

- The changing requirements in the type and level of knowledge, skills and competencies for today's knowledge-based economies and the insufficient opportunities to access higher levels of learning, including for the acquisition of knowledge and skills on ICT ("e-literacy"), especially in developing/low-income countries, are resulting in a knowledge divide, with major economic and employment consequences in today's mainly technology-driven world. (UNESCO, 2014, p. 1).

While these basic skills are important for individual participation in modern economies, the discussion here focuses mostly on the aggregate implications of the cognitive skills of a nation's workforce. Where significant proportions of the population have limited skills, economies are generally bound to employ production technologies that lag the best in both emerging and advanced economies. They also have more limited ability to innovate or even to imitate the possibilities that are found near the economic production frontier.

In simplest terms, countries with less-skilled populations – with less knowledge capital – will find it difficult to introduce productivity improvements. As a result, they will find economic growth and development to be slower. Finally, what growth there is will be less inclusive, because those without basic skills will be unable to keep pace with their more-skilled peers.

Cognitive skills are of fundamental importance for developing and advanced economies. Thus development goals built around basic skills have meaning to all societies around the world. They correct the distorted picture of the challenges facing the world suggested by the original Millennium Development Goals and the Education for All initiative, which framed the issue of education and skills as relevant to developing countries only. The challenges have clearly been more severe for less-developed economies, but they were and are real for more developed economies as well.

Structure of the report

This analysis begins with a short overview of the importance of knowledge capital for economic growth (Chapter 2).[5] Existing research shows that there has historically been a strong and direct relationship between the cognitive skills of national populations, measured by international tests of mathematics and science achievement, and countries' long-run growth. Moreover, this evidence provides strong reason to believe that the relationship is causal, i.e. if a nation improves the skills of its population, it can expect to grow faster. The analysis builds upon these historical findings in order to describe the potential economic improvements that would result from achieving a set of development goals that is based on expanding the knowledge capital of individual countries.

The somewhat abstract idea of knowledge capital is then put into the context of individual countries. After defining basic skills in terms of scores on the most recent installments of the major international student achievement tests – the OECD Programme for International Student Assessment (PISA) and the Trends in International Mathematics and Science Study (TIMSS) (Chapter 3) – it is possible to provide a comprehensive picture of knowledge capital for each of the 76 countries that have relevant data (Chapter 4).[6]

Of course, these tests do not provide a complete view of every country's youth. Some countries have not participated in international tests, so they cannot be directly compared with others, although participation in regional tests in Latin America and Africa provides information for a larger set of countries. Even in countries that do participate, the proportion of students who have already left school – and who are therefore out of the view of international testing – varies. Acknowledging those limitations, the report provides a country-by-country picture of the knowledge capital for as many countries as possible, and with as much completeness and accuracy as possible.

The heart of the analysis offers a concise economic perspective on a development goal – bringing all youth up to basic skills – defined in terms of the knowledge capital of nations (Chapter 5). This can be considered a fundamental development goal – the goal that makes it also possible to address the broader development goals. This fundamental goal emphasises the importance of skills over mere school attendance.

But of course young people are unlikely to develop appropriate skills without attending school, and this analysis builds upon the prior development goals related to access to schools. The analysis extends the simple cognitive skills goal to include schooling for all along with basic skills for all.

The past record on the interplay between cognitive skills and economic growth provides a means of estimating the economic gains from meeting the development goal set out in this report.[7] The economic benefit from reaching the development goal is calculated as the difference in future GDP with universal basic skills versus GDP with the country's current knowledge capital. Indeed, it is possible to provide these estimates on a country-by-country basis, at least for the 76 countries with current information on their knowledge capital and on the state of their aggregate economy.

Different scenarios are considered for policy outcomes and the impact of each one on economic outcomes is then estimated. In magnitude, the returns to universal basic skills are multiples of the current GDP in all countries in the world, including the countries with the highest income levels. The analysis shows that even for those developing countries that are far from achieving full enrolment in secondary schools, there are greater gains from improving school quality than from expanding enrolment in schools as they are.

Finally, in a somewhat more speculative analysis, the development goals are translated into a partial picture of how improvements in knowledge capital promote inclusiveness (Chapter 6). Bringing youth up to basic modern skills implies improved economic futures in particular *for the affected youth*. Existing information on the returns to skills in the labour market allows for some estimates, albeit partial, of how an improvement in skills achieves the complementary goal of bringing the rewards of economic development to a broader segment of society.

NOTES

1. The term "knowledge capital" is used to connote the aggregate cognitive skills of a country's population. The relevant skills for economic development, as discussed in this report, can be measured by international assessments, such as the Programme for International Student Assessment (PISA). See the broader discussion in Hanushek and Woessmann (2015).

2. Others have previously considered development goals that emphasise skills. Filmer, Hasan and Pritchett (2006) propose Millennium Learning Goals that are closely related to the goals described in this report. This argument is expanded with an in-depth analysis of learning profiles in developing countries by Pritchett (2013). The emphasis differs, however, by focusing on the economic benefits that accrue to a broad array of countries that meet alternative goals.

3. Other factors also enter into long-term growth. Importantly, as discussed in Chapter 5, the quality of economic institutions, such as having an open economy and having secure property rights, both influence growth and interact with the use of a country's knowledge capital. The skills of the population nonetheless remain strong and central to growth, even in the face of different economic institutions.

4. The operationalisation of this skill level relates directly to concepts and definitions in PISA, the OECD's international testing in mathematics, science and reading. In terms of PISA scores in mathematics, this means mastering at least Level 1, as is discussed in the next section. See also the descriptions in OECD (2013).

5. This discussion relies heavily on the analysis presented in Hanushek and Woessmann (2015).

6. PISA and TIMSS data are used. While there are test data for 81 countries or regions, sufficient economic data are missing for five.

7. This analysis elaborates on and extends the prior analysis of gains for OECD countries in OECD, Hanushek and Woessmann (2010).

REFERENCES

Filmer, D., A. Hasan and L. Pritchett (2006), "A Millennium Learning Goal: Measuring real progress in education", *Working Paper*, No. 97, August, Center for Global Development, Washington, DC.

Hanushek, E.A. and L. Woessmann (2015), *The Knowledge Capital of Nations: Education and the Economics of Growth*, The MIT Press, Cambridge, MA.

OECD (2013), *PISA 2012 Results: What Students Know and Can Do (Volume I, Revised edition, February 2014): Student Performance in Mathematics, Reading and Science*, OECD Publishing, Paris, http://dx.doi.org/10.1787/9789264208780-en.

OECD, E.A. Hanushek and L. Woessmann (2010), *The High Cost of Low Educational Performance: The Long-run Economic Impact of Improving PISA Outcomes*, PISA, OECD Publishing, Paris, http://dx.doi.org/10.1787/9789264077485-en.

Pritchett, L. (2013), *The Rebirth of Education: Schooling ain't Learning*, Center for Global Development, Washington, DC.

UNESCO (2014), Position paper on education post-2015, April 7, United Nations Educational, Scientific and Cultural Organization, Paris.

Chapter 2

Relationship between skills and economic growth

This chapter introduces the research on the connection between economic growth and the skills of a population, and briefly discusses some of the difficulties and uncertainties encountered in making this connection.

The process of economic growth has interested economists for much of the past century, but until recent decades, most studies remained as theory with little empirical work. Over the past 25 years, economists have linked the analysis much more closely to empirical observations and, in the process, rediscovered the importance of growth. The analysis, mirroring much of the recent empirical work, concentrates on the measurement of human capital and its role in describing why some countries have grown faster than others.

The existing empirical analysis of growth is now extensive, but this work has not always been convincing or successful. Extracting the fundamental factors underlying growth differences has proven difficult. This report builds on prior analysis by the authors that resolves the most important uncertainties in understanding long-run growth (Hanushek and Woessmann, 2015). That analysis shows that growth is directly and significantly related to the skills of the population. The key is measuring skills properly. In that work, as below, skills are measured by the aggregate test scores on international mathematics and science tests. The conclusion is that a population's knowledge capital, or collective cognitive skills, is by far the most important determinant of a country's economic growth.

Perhaps the easiest way to see the relationship is to plot the marginal impact of knowledge capital on long-run growth. Figure 2.1 depicts the fundamental association graphically, plotting annual growth in real per capita GDP between 1960 and 2000 against average test scores, after allowing for differences in initial per capita GDP and initial average years of schooling. Countries align closely along the regression line that depicts the positive association between cognitive skills and economic growth.[1]

FIGURE 2.1 KNOWLEDGE CAPITAL AND ECONOMIC GROWTH RATES ACROSS COUNTRIES

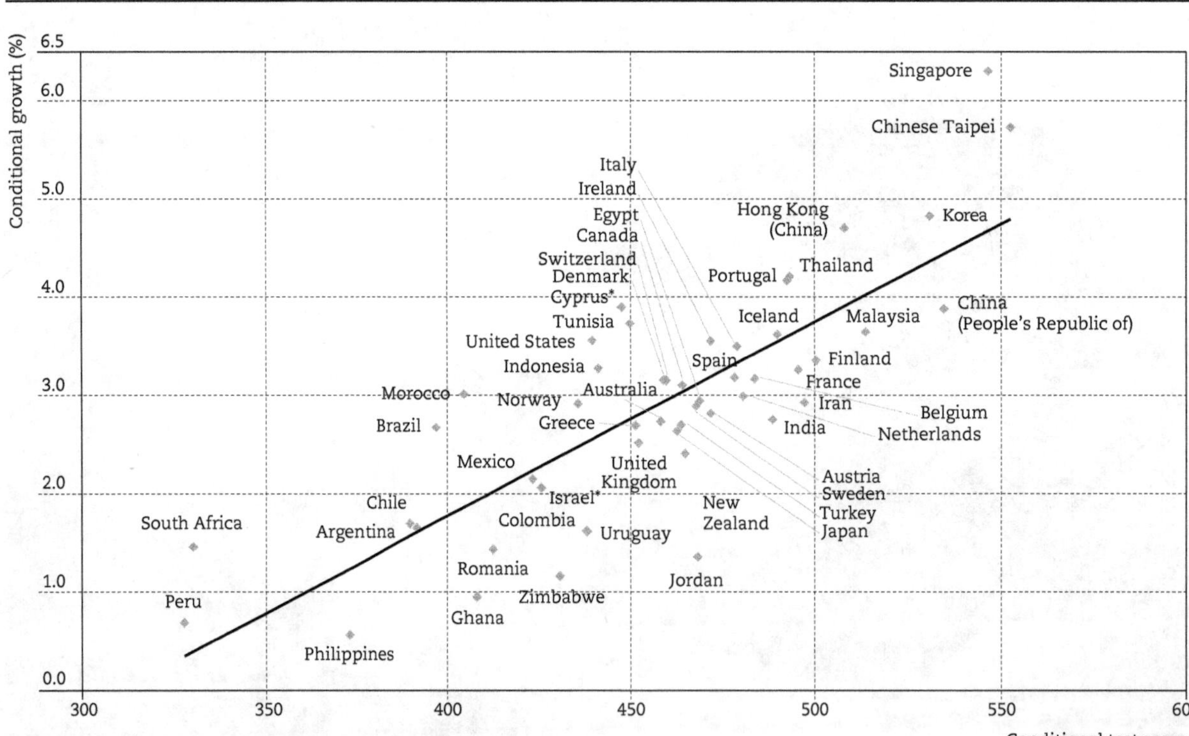

* See notes at the end of this chapter.

Notes: Added-variable plot of a regression of the average annual rate of growth (in %) of real per capita GDP from 1960 to 2000 on average test scores on international student achievement tests, average years of schooling in 1960, and initial level of real per capita GDP in 1960 (mean of unconditional variables added to each axis).

Source: Hanushek and Woessmann (2015).

This basic relationship underlies the discussion of a development goal defined in terms of skills, and of the economic implications of meeting such a goal. The plausibility of using these estimates as the basis of projections into the future must also be considered. Virtually all past economic analyses of the long-run growth of countries have highlighted a role for human capital, but the validity and reliability of the empirical analysis have been open to question (Pritchett, 2006). There have been concerns about the instability of estimates, which has been seen as evidence of mis-specified relationships that likely omit the influence of other factors. There has also been concern about reverse causality – i.e. the possibility that growth causes expansion of schooling rather than the opposite. As summarised in Annex A and laid out in detail in Hanushek and Woessmann (2015), these prior concerns can be satisfactorily answered once skills are correctly measured, and the basic growth relationships can support a detailed analysis of the economic implications of improving a nation's knowledge capital.

While the complete analysis of these statistical and modeling issues can be complicated, a summary is provided in Annex A, with appropriate references to more detailed analysis.

NOTES

1. The statistical model underlying Figure 2.1 is displayed in Annex Table A1 (column 3).

REFERENCES

Hanushek, E.A., and L.Woessmann (2015), *The Knowledge Capital of Nations: Education and the Economics of Growth*, The MIT Press, Cambridge, MA.

Pritchett, L. (2006), "Does learning to add up add up? The returns to schooling in aggregate data", in E.A. Hanushek and F. Welch (eds.), *Handbook of the Economics of Education*, North Holland, Amsterdam, pp. 635-695.

Notes regarding Cyprus

Readers should note the following information provided by Turkey and by the European Union Member States of the OECD and the European Union regarding the status of Cyprus:

Note by Turkey

The information in this document with reference to "Cyprus" relates to the southern part of the Island. There is no single authority representing both Turkish and Greek Cypriot people on the Island. Turkey recognises the Turkish Republic of Northern Cyprus (TRNC). Until a lasting and equitable solution is found within the context of the United Nations, Turkey shall preserve its position concerning the "Cyprus issue".

Note by all the European Union member States of the OECD and the European Union

The Republic of Cyprus is recognised by all members of the United Nations with the exception of Turkey. The information in this document relates to the area under the effective control of the Government of the Republic of Cyprus.

Note regarding Israel

The statistical data for Israel are supplied by and under the responsibility of the relevant Israeli authorities. The use of such data by the OECD is without prejudice to the status of the Golan Heights, East Jerusalem and Israeli settlements in the West Bank under the terms of international law.

Chapter 3

The goal: Every young person acquires basic skills

This chapter defines the concept of "basic" skills and identifies the people to whom this goal applies: all young people, not just those who are enrolled in school.

The conclusion suggested by the analysis described in Chapter 2 – that improved knowledge capital increases economic growth – has great relevance for any development goal. It suggests that in order to engender inclusive and sustainable growth, any goal must relate directly to populations' skills. Relevant goals should be phrased in terms of student achievement levels that are consistent with the skills required by the workforce in the future. This chapter defines these skills and what they entail.

The definition uses the OECD categories of performance, in part because these categories relate to the effective levels of skills in high-income economies. The definition refers to the skills of 15-year-old students who are enrolled in roughly the ninth year of schooling. Not only is this benchmark consistent with the Programme for International Student Assessment (PISA) testing that now covers a wide spectrum of countries, it also incorporates a school-enrolment component that builds on the original Millennium Development Goals and the Education for All aspirations for 2015.

Level 1 skills (fully attained) are assumed to represent the basic skills necessary for participating productively in modern economies.[1] The border line between Levels 1 and 2 is 420 points on the PISA mathematics scale.[2] With the mean of 500 and standard deviation of 100 for OECD countries, this score implies performance at the 23rd percentile of the OECD distribution. The OECD considers reaching Level 2 as "baseline skills", since these skills both open up further learning opportunities and prepare individuals for participation in modern market economies.

The different levels of performance correspond to distinct skills of individuals (OECD, 2013). The descriptions of the performance levels for mathematics are as follows:

LEVEL 1

At Level 1, students can answer questions involving familiar contexts where all relevant information is present and the questions are clearly defined. They are able to identify information and to carry out routine procedures according to direct instructions in explicit situations. They can perform actions that are almost always obvious and follow immediately from the given stimuli.

LEVEL 2

At Level 2, students can interpret and recognise situations in contexts that require no more than direct inference. They can extract relevant information from a single source and make use of a single representational mode. Students at this level can employ basic algorithms, formulae, procedures, or conventions to solve problems involving whole numbers. They are capable of making literal interpretations of the results.

In order to make these abstract explanations somewhat more concrete, Annex E gives a number of examples of questions that exemplify the skills required to successfully complete Level 1. The standard is that somebody with basic skills can reliably answer these questions and others like it, while somebody without basic skills cannot.

These skills clearly are not overly advanced – e.g. being able to convert from one currency to another with a known exchange rate, or to interpret a simple table of values for different products – but instead represent the kinds of problems routinely faced in a modern economy. As shown in subsequent chapters, significant proportions of young people in both high- and lower-income countries are unable to demonstrate this level of skill. Thus, reaching this skill level universally presents a tangible goal for all parts of the world.

The goal of ensuring basic skills for all should not be taken as defining a rigid cutoff of what modern technology requires. For an individual, being above this level is not "success" and below "failure." It is clear that there is a continuum of skills, and more is better than less for both individuals and society. Economies where the entire population exceeds the Level 1 standard will be better off in terms of growth than those that just get to this level. At the same time, these basic skills are heavily demanded throughout modern societies, and inclusive growth is difficult if there are substantial proportions of the population that lack the skills to participate fully in the economy.

This goal applies to all youth, not just those in school. Thus the routine testing of students in school, such as conducted by both PISA and the Trends in International Mathematics and Science Study (TIMSS), will provide a mistaken view of a country's actual achievement, since some young people will have already left the education system (and, on average, will presumably have lower skill levels than those still in school). This is not a serious issue in countries where school participation at age 15 is nearly universal; but it is a concern for the countries where a very large share of young people may leave school early.

Improving in PISA: Brazil

With an economy that traditionally relied on the extraction of natural resources and suffered stagnating growth and spells of hyperinflation until the early 1990s, Brazil is today rapidly expanding its industrial and service sector. Its population of more than 190 million, which is spread across 27 states in geographic areas as vast and diverse as Rio de Janeiro and the Amazon River basin, recognises the critical role education plays in the country's economic development.

As in only a handful of other countries, Brazil's performance in mathematics, reading and science has improved notably over the past decade. Its mean score in the PISA mathematics assessment has improved by an average of 4.1 point per year – from 356 points in 2003 to 391 points in 2012. Since 2000, reading scores have improved by an average of 1.2 score points per year; and, since 2006, science scores have risen by an average of 2.3 score points per year. Lowest-achieving students (defined as the 10% of students who score the lowest) have improved their performance by 65 score points – the equivalent of more than a year and a half of schooling. Despite these considerable improvements, around two out of three Brazilian students still perform below Level 2 in mathematics (in 2003, three in four students did).

Not only have most Brazilian students remarkably improved their performance, Brazil has expanded enrolment in primary and secondary schools. While in 1995, 90% of students were enrolled in primary schools at age seven, only half of them continued to finish eighth grade. In 2003, 35% of 15-year-olds were not enrolled in school in grade 7 or above; by 2012 this percentage had shrunk to 22%. Enrolment rates for 15-year-olds thus increased, from 65% in 2003 to 78% in 2012. Many of the students who are now included in the school system come from rural communities or socio-economically disadvantaged families, so the population of students who participated in the PISA 2012 assessment is very different from that of 2003.

PISA compares the performance of 15-year-old students who are enrolled in schools; but for those countries where this population has changed dramatically in a short period of time, trend data for students with similar background characteristics provide another way of examining how students' performance is changing beyond changes in enrolment. The table below compares the performance of students with similar socio-economic status across all years. The score attained by a socio-economically advantaged/average/disadvantaged student increased by 21/25/27 points, respectively, between 2003 and 2012.

OBSERVED AND EXPECTED TRENDS IN MATHEMATICS PERFORMANCE FOR BRAZIL (2003-12)

	2003		2012		Change between 2003 and 2012 (2012 – 2003)	
Total number of 15-year-olds	3 618 332		3 574 928		-43 404	
Total 15-year-olds enrolled in grades 7 or higher	2 359 854		2 786 064		+426 210	
Enrolment rates for 15-year-old students	65%		78%		+19%	
	Mean	**S.E.**	**Mean**	**S.E.**	**Mean**	**S.E.**
Mathematics performance	**356**	**(4,8)**	**391**	**(2,1)**	**+35.4**	**(5,6)**
Comparing the performance of students with similar socio-economic backgrounds:						
Advantaged student in 2003	383	(5,2)	404	(2,3)	+20.5	(6,0)
Average student in 2003	357	(4,0)	382	(1,6)	+24.9	(4,7)
Disadvantaged student in 2003	342	(3,9)	369	(1,7)	+27.3	(4,7)
Average performance excluding newly enrolled students assuming that newly enrolled students are at:						
Bottom half of performance	356	(4,8)	406	(2,2)	+49.7	(5,6)
Bottom quarter of performance	356	(4,8)	412	(2,0)	+56.4	(5,6)
Bottom of the distribution	356	(4,8)	415	(1,8)	+58.6	(5,5)
Average performance excluding newly enrolled students assuming that newly enrolled students come from:						
Bottom half of ESCS	356	(4,8)	397	(2,2)	+40.5	(5,7)
Bottom quarter of ESCS	356	(4,8)	399	(2,3)	+43.5	(5,7)
Bottom of ESCS	356	(4,8)	400	(2,3)	+44.1	(5,7)

Notes: Enrolment rates are those reported as the coverage index 3 in Annex A3 in the 2003 PISA Report (OECD, 2004) and in Annex A2 of this volume. An advantaged/disadvantaged student is one who has a PISA *index of economic, social and cultural status* (ESCS) that places him/her at the top/lower end of the fourth/first quartile of ESCS in 2003. Average students are those with an ESCS equal to the average in 2003. Average performance in 2012 that excludes newly enrolled students assuming that they come from the bottom half/quarter of performance and ESCS is calculated by randomly deleting 19% of the sample only among students scoring bottom half/quarter in the performance and ESCS distribution, respectively. Average performance in 2012 that excludes the bottom of the performance or ESCS distribution excludes the bottom 19% of the sample in the performance and ESCS distribution, respectively.

Improving in PISA: Brazil (continued)

The figure also simulates alternate scenarios, assuming that the students who are now enrolled in schools – but probably weren't in 2003 – score in the bottom half of the performance distribution, the bottom quarter of the performance distribution, or the bottom of the distribution and also come from the bottom half, bottom quarter, and bottom of the socio-economic distribution. Given that they assume that the newly enrolled students have lower scores than students who would have been enrolled in 2003, these simulations indicate the upper bounds of Brazil's improvement in performance.

For example, under the assumption that the newly enrolled students perform in the bottom quarter of mathematics performance, Brazil's improvement in mathematics, had enrolment rates retained their 2003 levels, would have been 56 score points. Similarly, if the assumption is that newly enrolled students come from the bottom quarter of the socio-economic distribution, Brazil's improvement in mathematics between 2003 and 2012 would have been 44 score points had enrolment rates not increased since 2003. Still, it is the observed enrolment rates and the observed performance in 2003 and 2012 that truly reflect the student population, its performance and the education challenges facing Brazil.

Brazil's increases in coverage are remarkable. However, although practically all students aged 7-14 start school at the beginning of the year, few continue until the end. They leave because the curriculum isn't engaging, or because they want or need to work, or because of the prevalence of grade repetition. The pervasiveness of grade repetition in Brazil has been linked to high dropout rates, high levels of student disengagement, and the more than 12 years it takes students, on average, to complete eight grades of primary school. (PISA results suggest that repetition rates remain high in Brazil: in 2003, 33% of students reported having repeated at least one grade in primary or secondary education; in 2012, 36% of students reported so).

Reform at the national level

Despite the fact that primary and secondary education is managed and largely funded at the municipal and state levels, the central government has been a key actor in driving and shaping education reform. Over the past 15 years it has actively promoted reforms to increase funding, improve teacher quality, set national curriculum standards, improve high school completion rates, develop and put in place accountability measures, and set student achievement and learning targets for schools, municipalities and states.

After Brazil's economy stabilised, in the mid-1990s, the Cardoso administration increased federal spending on primary education through FUNDEF (*Fundo de Manutenção e Desenvolvimento do Ensino Fundamental*) and simultaneously distributed the funding more equitably, replacing a population-density formula that allocated the majority of funds to large cities and linking part of the funding to school enrolments. This was only possible after developing a student and school census to gather and consolidate information about schools and students. FUNDEF also raised teachers' salaries, increased the number of teachers, increased the length of teacher-preparation programmes, and contributed to higher enrolments in rural areas. A conditional cash-transfer programme for families who send their 7-14 year-old children to school (Bolsa Escola) lifted many families out of subsistence-level poverty encouraging their interest that their children receive an education.

In 2006, the Lula administration expanded FUNDEF to cover early childhood and after-school learning and increased overall funding for education, renaming the programme FUNDEB, as it now covered basic education more broadly. The administration also expanded the conditional cash transfers to cover students aged 15-17, thereby encouraging enrolment in upper secondary education, where enrolment is lowest. This expansion means that 6.1% of Brazil's GDP is now spent on education and the country aims to devote 10% of its GDP to education by 2020. Funding for this important increase in education expenditure will come from the recently approved allocation of 75% of public revenues from oil to education.

Improving the quality of teachers

A core element of FUNDEF was increasing teacher salaries, which rose 13% on average after FUNDEF, and more than 60% in the poorer, northeast region of the country. At the same time, the 1996 Law of Directive and Bases of National Education (LDB) mandated that, by 2006, all new teachers have a university qualification, and that initial and in-service teacher training programmes be free of charge. These regulations came at a time when coverage was expanding significantly, leading to an increase in the number of teachers in the system. In 2000, for example, there were 430 467 secondary school teachers, and 88% of whom had a tertiary degree; in 2012 there were 497 797 teachers, 95% of whom had tertiary qualifications (INEP, 2000 and 2012). Subsequent reforms in the late 2000s sought to create standards for teachers' career paths based on qualifications, not solely on tenure. The planned implementation of a new examination system for teacher certification, covering both content and pedagogy, has been delayed. Although universities are free to determine their curriculum for teacher-training programmes, the establishment of an examination system to certify teachers sends a strong signal of what content and pedagogical orientation should be developed.

Improving in PISA: Brazil (continued)

To encourage more students to enrol – and stay – in school, upper secondary education has become mandatory (this policy is being phased in so that enrolment will be obligatory for students aged 4 to 17 by 2016), and a new grade level has been added at the start of primary school. Giving students more opportunities to learn in school has also meant shifting to a full school day, as underscored in the 2011-2020 National Plan for Education. Most school days are just four hours long; and even though FUNDEB provided incentives for full-day schools, they were not sufficient to prompt the investments in infrastructure required for schools that accommodate two or three shifts in a day to become full-day schools. Although enrolment in full-day schools increased 24% between 2010 and 2012, overall coverage in full-day schools remains low: only 2 million out of a total of almost 30 million students attended such schools in 2012 (INEP, 2013).

The reforms of the mid-1990s included provisions to improve the education information system and increase school accountability. It transformed the National Institute for Educational Studies and Research into an independent organisation responsible for the national assessment and evaluation of education. It turned a national assessment system into the Evaluation System for Basic Education (SAEB/Prova Brazil) for grades 4, 8 and 11 and the National Secondary Education Examination in Grade 11, which provides qualifications for further studies or entry into the labour market. SAEB changed over time to become a national census-based assessment for students in grades 4 and 8 and its results were combined with repetition and dropout rates in 2005 to create an index of schools quality, the Basic Education Development Index (IDEB). This gave schools, municipalities and states an incentive to reduce retention and dropout rates and a benchmark against which to monitor their progress. The IDEB is set individually for each school and is scaled so that its levels are aligned with those of PISA. Results are widely published, and schools that show significant progress are granted more autonomy while schools that remain low performers are given additional assistance. Support for schools is also offered through the Fundescola programme. IDEB provides targets for each school; it is up to the schools, municipalities and states to develop strategic improvement plans. In line with Brazil's progress in PISA, national performance as measured by the SAEB has also improved between 1999 and 2009 (Bruns, Evans and Luque, 2011).

Perhaps as a result of these reforms, not only are more Brazilian students attending school and performing at higher levels, they are also attending better-staffed schools (the index of teacher shortage dropped from 0.47 in 2003 to 0.19 in 2012, and the number of students per teacher in a school fell from 34 to 28 in the same period), and schools with better material resources (the index of quality of educational resources increased from -1.17 to -0.54). They are also attending schools with better learning environments, as shown by improved disciplinary climates and student-teacher relations. Students in 2012 also reported spending one-and-a-half hours less per week on homework than their counterparts in 2003 did.

Sources:

Bruns, B., D. Evans and J. Luque (2011), *Achieving World-Class Education in Brazil*, The World Bank, Washington, D.C.

Instituto Nacional de Estudos e Pesquisas Educacionais Anísio Teixeira (INEP) (2000), *Sinopse Estatística da Educação Básica 2000*, INEP, Brasilia.

Instituto Nacional de Estudos e Pesquisas Educacionais Anísio Teixeira (INEP) (2012), *Sinopse Estatística da Educaçao Básica 2012*, INEP, Brasilia.

Instituto Nacional de Estudos e Pesquisas Educacionais Anísio Teixeira (INEP) (2013), *Censo da Educação Básica: 2012, Resumo Técnico*, INEP, Brasilia.

OECD (2011), *OECD Economic Surveys: Brazil 2011*, OECD Publishing, Paris. http://dx.doi.org/10.1787/eco_surveys-bra-2011-en

OECD (2010), *Lessons from PISA for the United States*, Strong Performers and Successful Reformers in Education, OECD Publishing, Paris. http://dx.doi.org/10.1787/9789264096660-en

NOTES

1. Filmer, Hasan and Pritchett (2006) arrive at the same standard when they develop their Millennium Learning Goals.

2. Note that the border between Levels 1 and 2 in science is slightly lower at 407 points (OECD, 2013). Nonetheless, 420 PISA points are used for both mathematics and science.

REFERENCES

Filmer, D., A. Hasan and L. Pritchett (2006), "A Millennium Learning Goal: Measuring real progress in education", *Working Paper*, No. 97, August, Center for Global Development, Washington, DC.

OECD (2013), *PISA 2012 Results: What Students Know and Can Do (Volume I, Revised edition, February 2014): Student Performance in Mathematics, Reading and Science*, OECD Publishing, Paris, http://dx.doi.org/10.1787/9789264208780-en.

Chapter 4

Distance from the goal of basic skills for all

How far do countries have to go to achieve the goal of basic skills for all? This chapter offers a comprehensive picture of the current state of "knowledge capital" in each of the 76 countries that have relevant data. It also provides additional information about some of the countries in Latin America and sub-Saharan Africa that have not participated in either PISA or TIMSS, but have participated in regional assessments, and information concerning India and China.

To appreciate both the possibilities and the challenges that lie ahead, it is important to understand the current level of skills across countries. Previous assessments of the state of schooling around the world have relied heavily upon estimates of countries' rates of school attendance and completion.[1] While there has been growing recognition that quality and learning are not the same as school attendance, there is not yet a consistent measurement of the knowledge capital of nations.[2] This report splices together available information from international assessments to give the most comprehensive picture possible.

The starting point is comparative data for the 81 countries that have participated in the most recent mathematics and science assessments in either the Programme for International Student Assement (PISA) or the Trends in International Mathematics and Science Study (TIMSS). Most of these (65 countries) are consistently recorded in the PISA 2012 assessment of 15-year-olds. These data are combined with data for 16 additional countries that participated in the TIMSS 2011 assessment of eighth graders, but not in PISA. Combining data from the two tests is justified, since results for the two tend to be very similar. Among the 28 countries participating in both, the correlation of average achievement scores across the two tests is 0.944 in mathematics and 0.930 in science. All countries are placed on the PISA scale. (Annex B describes the methodology for combining the tests; Table B.1 lists the countries for which testing data are available and indicates whether data come from PISA or from TIMSS).[3]

Ultimately, the analysis includes the 76 countries with both assessment information and internationally comparable data on GDP.[4] These 76 countries accounted for 68.1% of world GDP and 36.9% of the world's population in 2013, according to estimates by the International Monetary Fund (IMF).[5]

Average achievement and lack of basic skills in participating countries

The simplest view of variations in knowledge capital across the 76 countries is found in Figure 4.1, which ranks the countries by their averaged mathematics and science test scores.

Twenty-one countries have average scores above 500, the OECD average in 2000. On average, Singapore is over 0.6 standard deviation above this mean. At the other end of the spectrum, students in Ghana are over two standard deviations below it. A rough rule of thumb from high-income countries is that, on average, students' test scores increase by about one-quarter to one-third of a standard deviation per year. Thus, average country differences of such magnitude among students who have spent the same amount of time in school indicate truly enormous learning differences across students in different countries. In other words, they indicate dramatic variations in countries' knowledge capital. Interestingly, average scores for low- and high-income countries show virtually no overlap; with few exceptions, the latter are significantly higher than the former.

FIGURE 4.1 AVERAGE PERFORMANCE ON INTERNATIONAL STUDENT ACHIEVEMENT TESTS

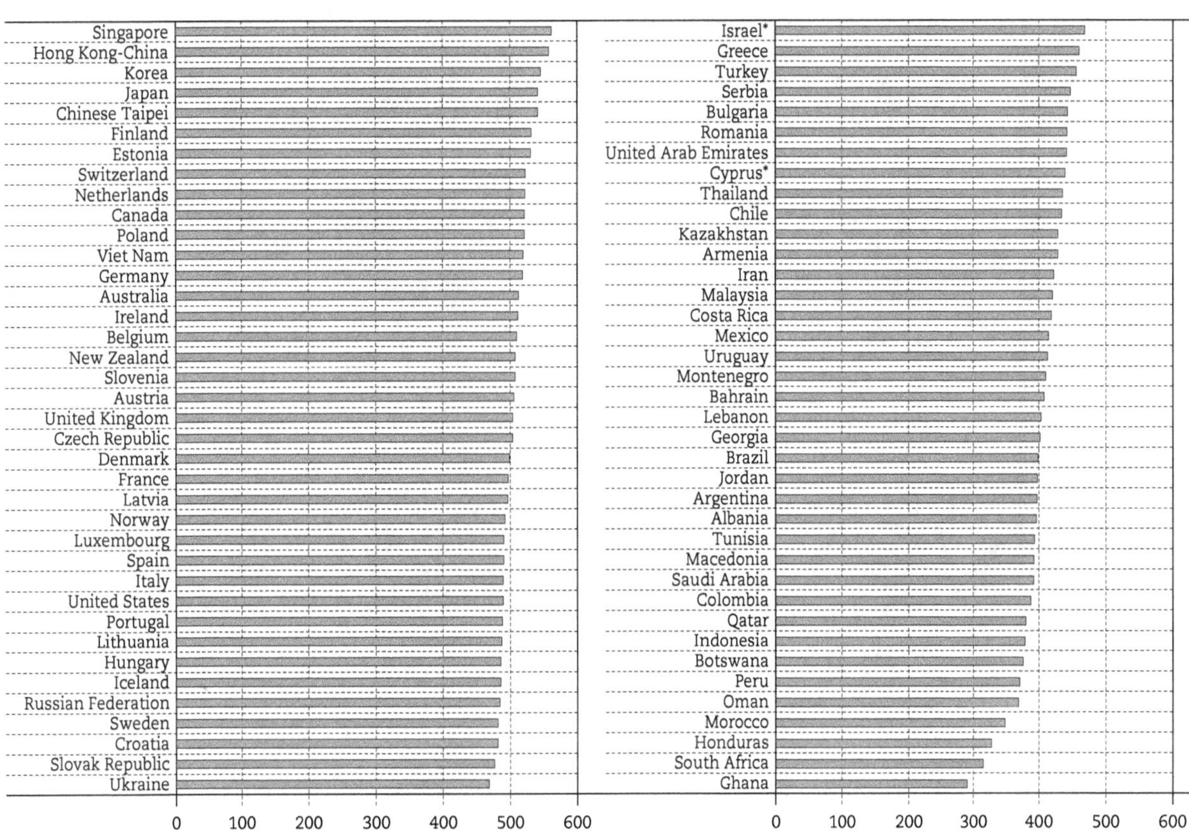

* See notes at the end of this chapter.

Notes: Average score on international student achievement tests. Average of mathematics and science. PISA participants: PISA 2012 score; TIMSS (non-PISA) participants: based on 8th-grade TIMSS 2011 micro data, transformed to PISA scale. See Annex B and Table B.1 for details.

In terms of the education development goals, of course, the interest centres on the population of each country that has not yet acquired basic skills. Figure 4.2 presents, for the 76 countries, the share of youth in school who fall below the level that indicates the acquisition of basic skills, that is, below 420 on the mathematics and science assessments. One might expect countries with higher average scores to have smaller shares of students without basic skills, and the ranking of countries in Figure 4.2 does look close to the mirror image of Figure 4.1, which shows the average scores (though in fact the rankings are slightly different). The correlation between the average score and the share of youth who score below 420 points is -0.989.

FIGURE 4.2 SHARE OF STUDENTS NOT ACQUIRING BASIC SKILLS

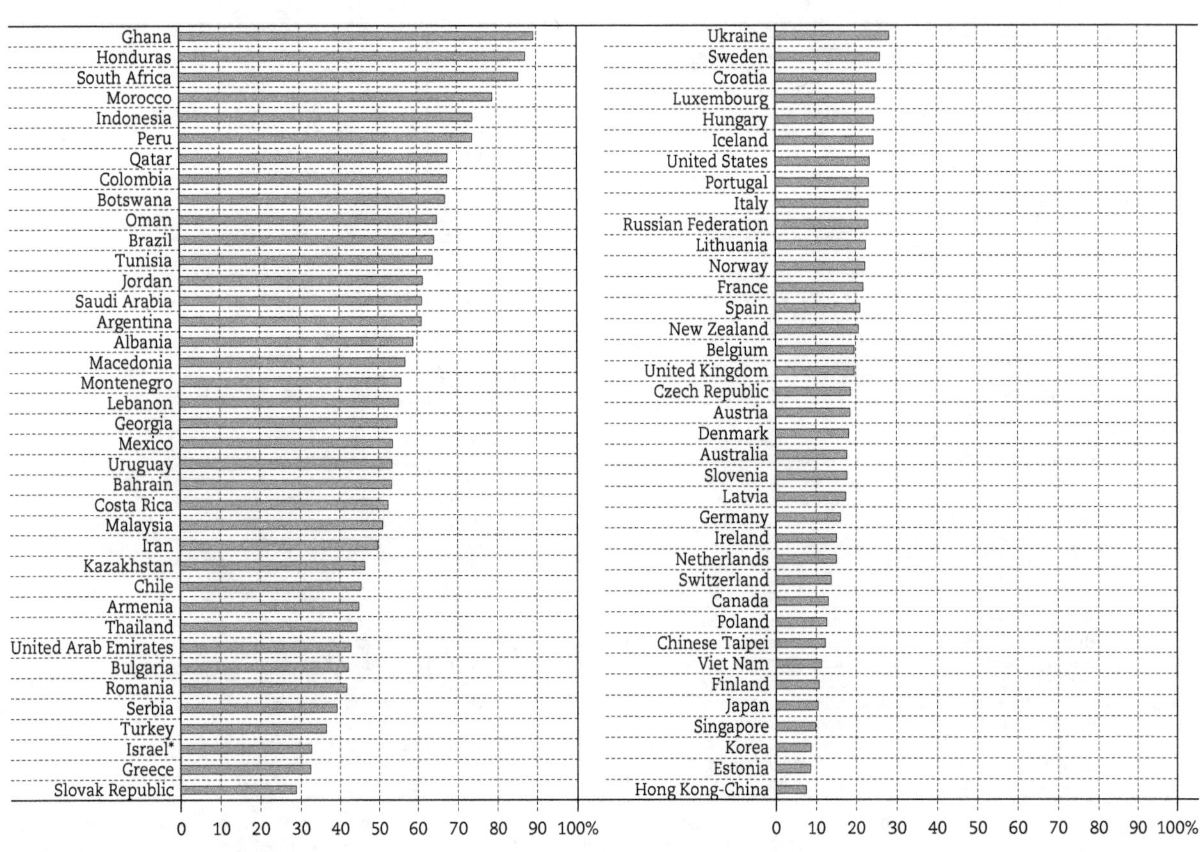

* See notes at the end of this chapter.

Notes: Share of students performing below 420 points on international student achievement test. Average of mathematics and science. PISA participants: based on PISA 2012 micro data; TIMSS (non-PISA) participants: based on 8th-grade TIMSS 2011 micro data, transformed to PISA scale. See Annex B and Table B.1 for details.

In 9 of the 76 countries (Ghana, Honduras, South Africa, Morocco, Indonesia, Peru, Qatar, Colombia and Botswana), more than two-thirds of students fail to meet the level of basic skills. Hong Kong-China, Estonia, Korea and Singapore lead at the other end of the distribution, but even these countries/economies face the challenge of ensuring that all youth attain basic skill levels. Even the richest countries in the world also have significant populations without basic skills: Luxembourg (25%), Norway (22%), the United States (24%) and Switzerland (14%). In other words, the development goal is significant and real for all of the countries in the world.

Improving in PISA: Korea

Korea has consistently performed at the top level in PISA, and has still improved over time. In PISA 2000, Korea performed on a par with New Zealand, Sweden, Australia, Hong Kong-China, Japan and Ireland; by 2012, Korea outperformed the first three. Performance in reading, for example, has improved by an average of almost one score point per year since 2000. As a result, Korea's average score in reading increased from 525 points in 2003 to 536 points in 2012. This improvement was concentrated at the top of the performance distribution: the percentage of students scoring at or above proficiency Level 5 in mathematics increased by more than eight percentage points since 2000 to 14% in 2012. While the mathematics scores among the top 10% of students have improved by more than 30 points during the period, no change was observed among low-achieving students. Korea's performance in science also improved consistently throughout its participation in PISA: science performance increased by an average of 2.6 points per year since 2006 so that average scores in science rose from 522 points in PISA 2006 to 538 points in PISA 2012.

Korea's improvements in reading were concentrated among high-achieving students. the average improvement of high-achieving students outpaced that of lower-achieving students. Higher standards in language literacy were put in place in the mid-2000s, and language literacy was given more weight in the competitive College Scholastic Ability Test (CSAT), the university entrance examination. This could explain the increase in the share of top-performing students in Korea, as high-achieving students have more incentives to invest in language and reading literacy. Also, and particularly since 2010, programmes for gifted students have been expanded at the primary and secondary levels, and the secondary curriculum has been strengthened to meet the needs of these students (MEST, 2010).

Education policies have been linked to macroeconomic development first through centralised planning (1962-91) then by co-ordinated and strategically oriented approaches through the National Human Resource Development Plans (one for 2001-05 and another for 2006-10, for example). They have followed a sequential approach. Prior to 1975, 65% of the education budget was spent on primary education; in the following decades, secondary education received a greater share of funding and by the late 1990s, public investment in tertiary education was expanded. In the mid-1990s, a comprehensive school reform was launched, introducing school deregulation, choice, a new curriculum and increased public expenditure. Individual schools began to assume more management responsibilities. By 2012, schools had greater autonomy, and programmes were specifically designed to assist school leaders in assuming their new roles (World Bank, 2010).

The National Assessment of Educational Achievement programme

The National Assessment of Educational Achievement (NAEA) programme was introduced in 1998. NAEA assesses educational achievement and trends among all 6th-, 9th- and 10th-grade students in Korean Language Arts, English, mathematics, social studies and science. Since 2010, the programme changed the grade coverage from 6th-, 9th- and 10th to 6th-, 9th- and 11th. The Subject Learning Diagnostic Test (SLDT) was introduced in 2008 and is implemented by the Nationwide Association of Superintendents of metropolitan/provincial offices of education. The previous Diagnostic Evaluation of Basic Academic Competence (DEBAC), which had tested primary school 3rd grades at the national level since 2002, was delegated to metropolitan/provincial offices of education. The Subject Learning Diagnostic Test measures basic competency in reading, writing and mathematics among 3rd-, 4th-, 5th-, 7th- and 8th-grade students. Through these assessment tools, the government and metropolitan/provincial offices can monitor individual student performance levels, establish achievement benchmarks, develop an accountability system for public education, and also identify students who need support. For example, in 2008, the government established the *Zero Plan for Below-Basic Students*, a national programme to ensure that all students meet basic achievement criteria. The NAEA assessment was converted from a sample-based test to a census-based test to identify and then support low-performing students. Also, MEST introduced a *Schools for Improvement* (SFI) policy in 2009 to provide support in closing education gaps and improving achievement, also with the aim of reducing the proportion of students who do not achieve basic proficiency. The SFI supports various education programmes, including providing more resources for low-income schools and schools with a high concentration of low-performing students (Kim et al., 2012).

The national curriculum was revised again in 2009, highlighting reasoning, problem solving and mathematical communication as key competencies in mathematics (MEST, 2011b). In 2012, the government announced a plan for improving mathematics education in keeping with the revised curriculum. The aim is to enhance skills in reasoning and creativity (MEST, 2012). This reform implies a profound change in the way teachers teach mathematics: up until now, teachers have largely taught to the CSAT.

Improving in PISA: Korea (continued)

Changes in the classroom

Reforms have also affected the teaching of language and reading. The focus of the Korean Language Arts Curriculum shifted from proficiency in grammar and literature to skills and strategies needed for creative and critical understanding and representation, similar to the approach underlying PISA. Diverse teaching methods and materials that reflected those changes were developed, and investments were made in related digital and Internet infrastructure. Schools were requested to spend a fixed share of their budgets on reading education. Training programmes for reading teachers were developed and disseminated. Parents were encouraged to participate more in school activities and were given information on how to support their children's schoolwork.

In both 2009 and 2012, Korea was among the OECD countries with the largest classes and, since 2003, Korean students have also been more likely to attend schools where the principal reported a teacher shortage. A concerted effort is underway to create more teaching posts. In 2010, more than 53 000 new jobs were assigned to the education-services sector, including 2 000 English conversation lecturers, 7 000 intern teachers, who support instruction, 7 000 after-school lecturers and co-ordinators, 5 500 full-day kindergarten staff, and 5 000 special education assistants. The teacher-training system has been expanded to enable outside experts to acquire teaching certificates (MEST, 2010; 2011a).

The school- and teacher-evaluation systems have also been reformed. Since 2010, the teacher-evaluation system, which was developed to improve teachers' professional capacities, was expanded to all schools. Results from the evaluation lead to customised training programmes for teachers, depending on their results. Given the greater autonomy granted to school principals, evaluation information will be made public and regional offices of education will oversee monitoring, focusing more on output-oriented criteria. Schools will use internal assessments to measure the improvement of students who do not meet the national assessment benchmarks. School-based performance-award systems were introduced in 2011 (MEST, 2011).

Fifteen-year-old students in Korea spent an average of 30 minutes less in mathematics classes in 2012 than their counterparts in 2003 did, yet a large number of Korean students participate in after-school lessons. While private lessons are common among those who can afford them, after-school group classes are often subsidised, so even disadvantaged students frequently enrol. For example, in June 2011, 99.9% of all primary and secondary schools were operating after-school programmes and about 65% of all primary and secondary students participated in after-school activities (MEST, 2011c). Many observers suspect that the high participation rates in after-school classes may be due to cultural factors and an intense focus on preparing for university entrance examinations. PISA 2006 data show that Korean students attending schools with socio-economically advantaged students are more likely to attend after-school lessons with private teachers than students in other countries; and disadvantaged students in Korea are more likely to attend after-school group lessons than disadvantaged students in other countries. In both cases, attendance in these lessons, along with other factors, is associated with better performance on PISA (OECD, 2010).

Sources:

Kim K. et al. (2012), *Korea-US bilateral study on turnaround schools* (CRE 2012-12-2). KICE, Seoul.

Ministry of Education, Science and Technology (2012), *Plans for advancing mathematics education* (in Korean), MEST, Seoul.

Ministry of Education, Science and Technology (2011a), *Major Policies and Plans for 2011*, MEST, Seoul.

Ministry of Education, Science and Technology (2011b), *Mathematical curriculum* (in Korean), MEST, Seoul.

Ministry of Education, Science and Technology (2011c), *2011 Analysis for after school programme* (in Korean), MEST, Seoul.

Ministry of Education, Science and Technology (2010), *Major Policies and Plans for 2010*, MEST, Seoul.

OECD (2011), *Quality Time for Students: Learning in and out of school*, PISA, OECD Publishing, Paris. http://dx.doi.org/10.1787/9789264087057-en

World Bank (2010), *Quality of Education in Colombia, Achievements and Challenges Ahead: Analysis of the Results of TIMSS 1995-2007*, World Bank, Washington, DC.

Achievement of other countries on regional tests

Can anything be said about the educational achievement in countries that did not participate in the PISA and TIMSS tests? It would be reasonable to suppose that participating countries have greater knowledge capital than non-participants. Indeed, there is ample evidence that in many developing countries that do not participate in international tests, a majority of students does not attain basic skills, despite spending considerable time in school (Prichett, 2013). But because they do not participate in the international assessments, it is difficult to determine the challenges these countries face. The following provides information about some of the countries in Latin America and sub-Saharan Africa that have not participated in either PISA or TIMSS as well as information concerning India and China.

LATIN AMERICA

Eight countries in Latin America participated in the PISA 2012 assessments, and only Chile (in 48th place) was among the 50 with the highest average scores. But performance in Latin American countries can also be observed through the regional testing in 2013 that included these eight countries plus an additional seven that did not participate in PISA. This regional assessment, called *Tercer Estudio Regional Comparativo y Explicativo* (TERCE), was the third for the region and provides information on mathematics performance among the slightly younger cohort of sixth graders.[6] The correlation among the eight participants in both TERCE and PISA is 0.86. In other words, the rankings of these countries based on TERCE scores are very similar to the rankings based on PISA scores. This similarity can be seen in Figure 4.3, which shows performance rankings on TERCE in sixth-grade mathematics interwoven with the PISA score (blue bars) for those countries participating in both.

None of the countries that did not participate in PISA scored above any of the participants – and the participants scored very poorly.[7] The additional information provided by the TERCE scores suggests that skill levels among all Latin American students are even lower than what the observed PISA scores suggest.

FIGURE 4.3 AVERAGE PERFORMANCE OF LATIN AMERICAN COUNTRIES ON INTERNATIONAL AND REGIONAL STUDENT ACHIEVEMENT TESTS

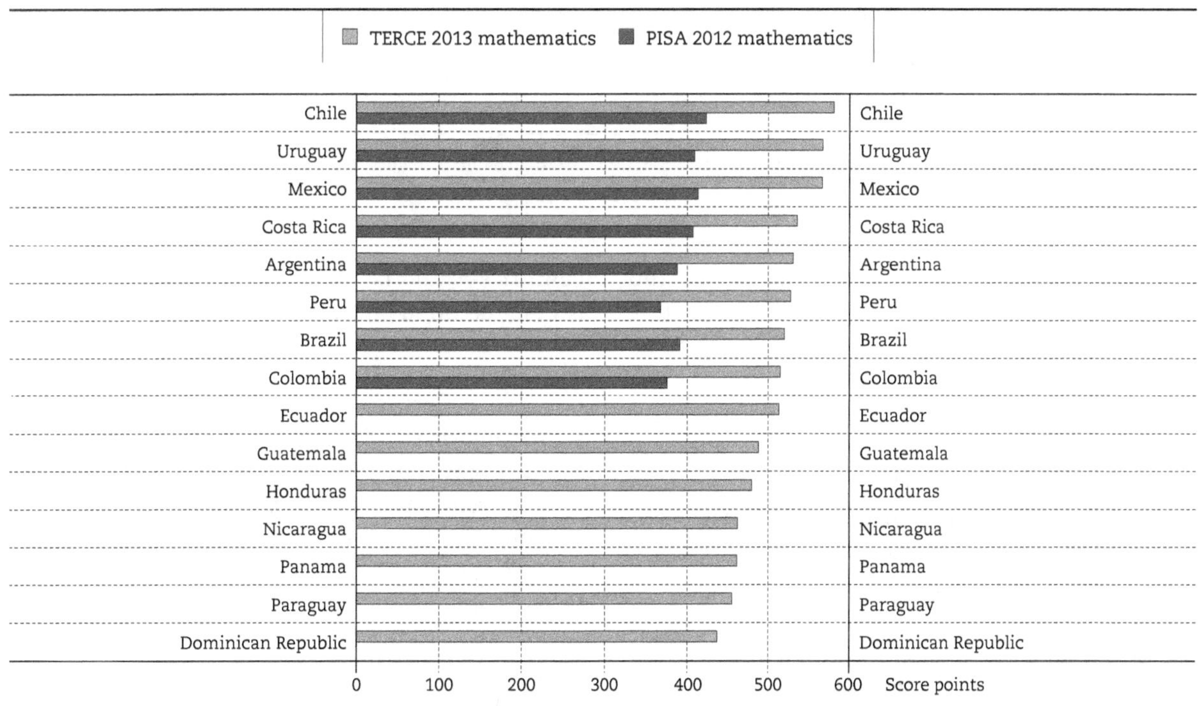

Notes: Average score on international student achievement test. TERCE: 6th-grade mathematics, 2013. PISA: 15-year-olds, mathematics, 2012.

SUB-SAHARAN AFRICA

A similar expansion of countries is possible for sub-Saharan Africa. The Southern and Eastern Africa Consortium for Monitoring Educational Quality (SACMEQ) has tested students in African countries at three different times. SACMEQ III provides information on sixth-grade mathematics in 15 African countries in 2007.[8]

Figure 4.4 ranks the SACMEQ countries by their mathematics scores in 2007. Also included in the figure is the regional ranking of Botswana and South Africa, which were 70th and 75th, respectively, on the international scale of PISA/TIMSS. Botswana and South Africa are two of the three countries, together with Honduras, that assessed ninth-graders in TIMSS because the assessment was deemed too difficult for eighth-graders. Thus, their international performance is likely to be overstated.

FIGURE 4.4 AVERAGE PERFORMANCE OF SUB-SAHARAN AFRICAN COUNTRIES ON INTERNATIONAL AND REGIONAL STUDENT ACHIEVEMENT TESTS

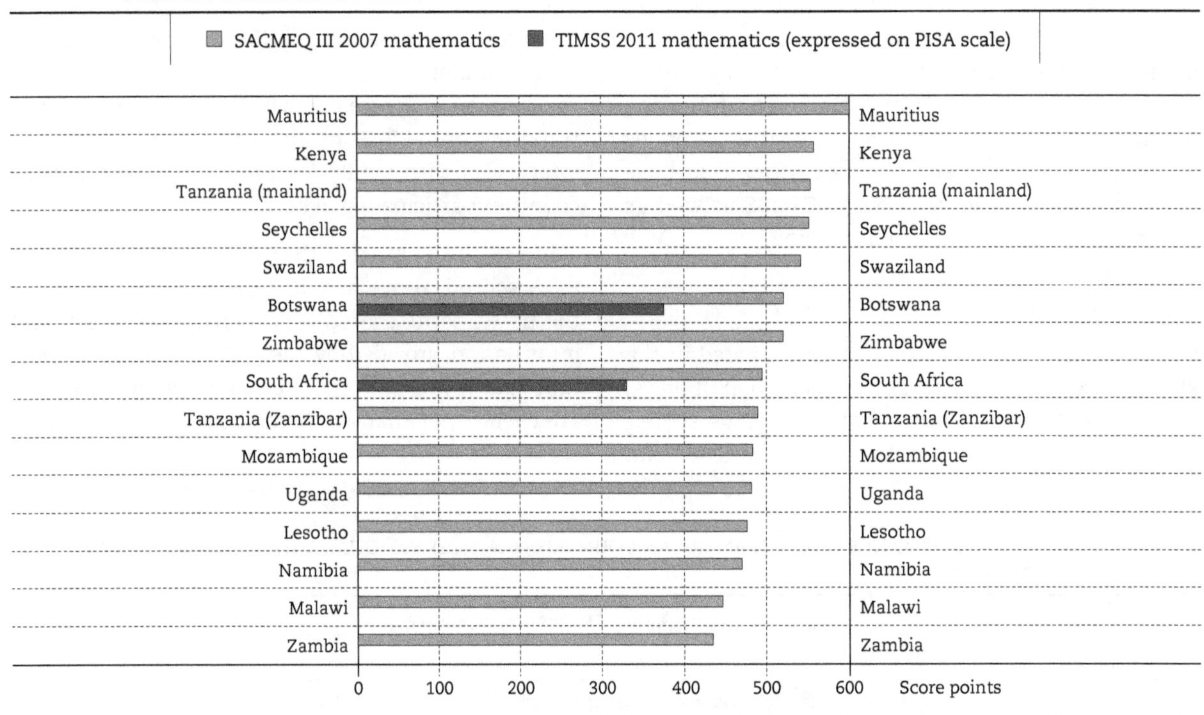

Notes: Average score on international student achievement test. SACMEQ III: 6th-grade mathematics, 2007. TIMSS: 9th-grade mathematics, 2011 (expressed on PISA scale, see Annex B for details).

Among the SACMEQ countries, Botswana and South Africa fall roughly in the middle, indicating that, contrary to the experience in Latin America, the countries not participating in the international tests are not uniformly on the bottom of the skills distribution. Nonetheless, the evidence does not suggest that the countries that have not participated in the international assessments are internationally competitive. While Mauritius is a full standard deviation ahead of Botswana on the SACMEQ III test, the other countries that have not participated in the international testing that outpace Botswana (Kenya, Tanzania, the Seychelles and Swaziland) are ahead by just 0.3 standard deviation. If this gain were carried over to the international scale (see Figure 4.1), these countries would fall somewhere between 55th and 60th in the world rankings.

The regional picture from just the participating countries' performance does not seem to have significantly biased the picture of African performance. But the key for development prospects is that participating countries are virtually at the bottom of the international achievement picture – and 7 of the 13 other participants on the regional test fall even below them.

INDIA

Comprehensive data for India are not available, but two Indian states participated in PISA in 2009:

Himachal Pradesh and Tamil Nadu.[9] The average mathematics and science performance of Himachal Pradesh is 331.8 points and that of Tamil Nadu is 349.6 points.[10] These scores place them (just) ahead of Kyrgyzstan (330.5 points), but below the other 63 PISA participants in 2009 – and below every one of the 64 PISA participants in 2012, when Peru scored the lowest (370.6 points).

The question, however, is where these states fall in the distribution of skills for India – that is, how representative they are for the country as a whole. Comprehensive data are not readily available, but the 2011 Census of India ranked Himachal Pradesh 11th and Tamil Nadu 14th in literacy among the country's 35 states and union territories.[11] In terms of poverty, Himachal Pradesh has the fourth lowest poverty rate and Tamil Nadu the tenth lowest. Thus, these states do not appear to be at the bottom of the education distribution in India.

Two other studies also show poor student performance in India. The first, by Das and Zajonc (2010), estimates rankings for two states (Orissa and Rajasthan) using released items from the TIMSS assessments. It concludes that "these two states fall below 43 of the 51 countries for which data exist. The bottom 5% of children rank higher than the bottom 5% in only three countries – South Africa, Ghana and Saudi Arabia."

The second study, the 2014 Annual Status of Education Report (Rural) for India, calls the results for basic reading "extremely disheartening." The report notes that in 2014, a quarter of third-graders, half of fifth-graders, and about three-quarters of eighth-graders could read at a second-grade level.[12] Judging from the eighth-grade results, the goal of having all students reach basic skills (Level 1) is a very distant one.[13]

CHINA

China has not participated in PISA or TIMSS, although there are PISA 2012 results available for Shanghai-China.[14] Shanghai's scores – 613 points in mathematics and 580 points in science – were higher than those of Singapore, the country ranked first among the 76 countries shown in Figure 4.1.

It is difficult to know how to generalise from these results. Shanghai is the wealthiest city in China and has attracted a very skilled labour force.

While a larger sample of other provinces have carried out PISA assessments on their own, their results have not been made public. Thus, it is not possible to generalise about the achievement levels for China as a whole.

School enrolment in participating countries

The provided score distributions, however, do not give the entire picture of countries' knowledge capital, since significant numbers of youth – particularly in lower-income countries – are not enrolled in school, and thus are not being tested. There is reason to be concerned about the number of countries that have yet to ensure broad access to and enrolment in secondary schools.

Figure 4.5 displays net enrolment rates at the tested age for each of the 76 countries in the test sample.[15] While 44 of the countries have over 95% participation of their 15-year-olds, the participation rates begin to fall significantly after this point. In the bottom 17 countries, less than 80% of 15-year-olds are enrolled.

The concern about low enrolment and its effect on knowledge capital is probably best illustrated by Viet Nam. On the 2012 PISA test, Viet Nam ranked 12th; moreover, less than 12% of tested Vietnamese students fell below the basic skills level of 420 points. Yet only 64% of Viet Nam's 15-year-olds were enrolled in school in 2012. Its enrolment rate is 74th among the 76 countries; only Botswana and Ghana have lower rates. Given its highly selected school population, it is impossible to conclude that Viet Nam is approaching the goal of basic skills for all.

Admittedly, Viet Nam is an exception. Most countries near the bottom on enrolment also tend to have low achievement. Ghana, for example, has the lowest achievement among young people in school of all 76 countries, while Botswana is 70th in the achievement rankings. In fact, the correlation between the average score and the enrolment rate in the 76-country sample is 0.659. Enrolment rates and achievement levels appear to be strongly and positively related, in general (Hanushek and Woessmann, 2011).

FIGURE 4.5 SECONDARY SCHOOL ENROLMENT RATES

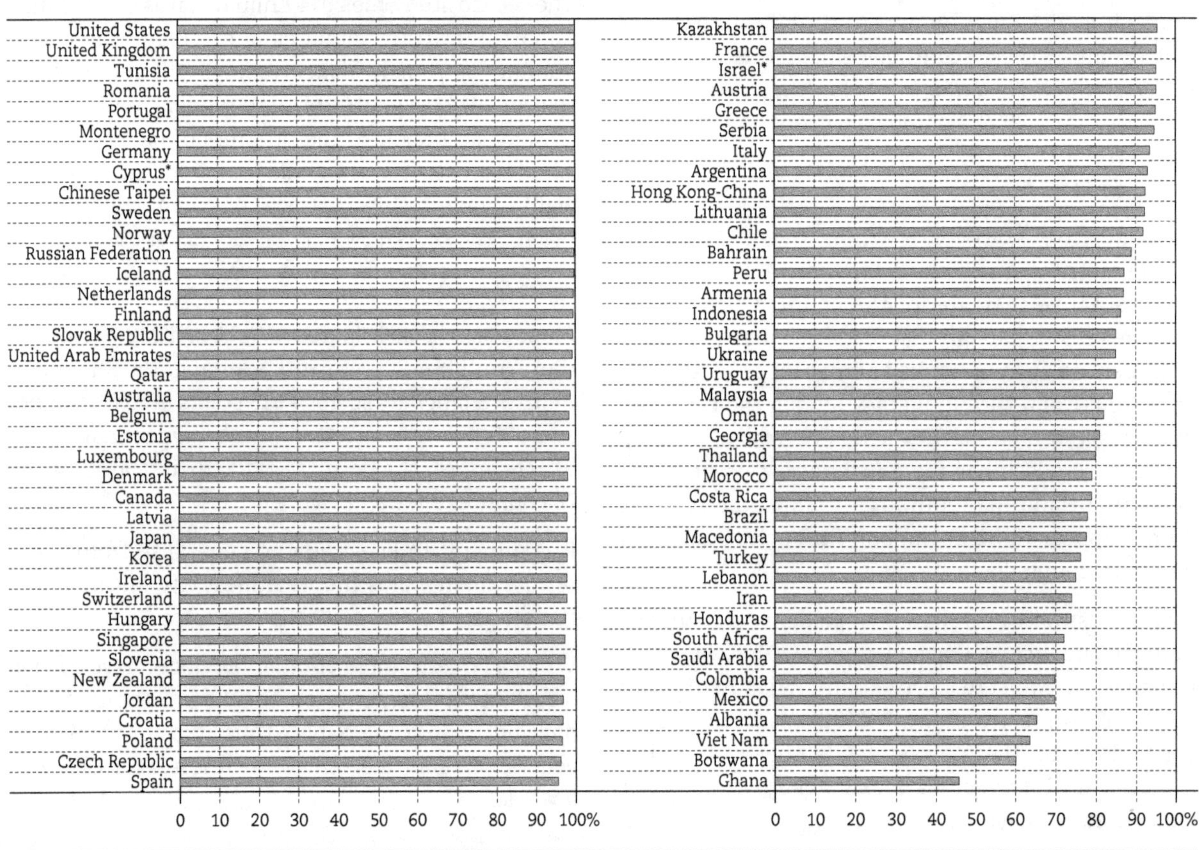

* See notes at the end of this chapter.

Notes: PISA participants: share of 15-year-olds enrolled in school; TIMSS (non-PISA) participants: net enrolment ratio in secondary education (% of relevant group).

The development challenge

Historically, development policy has sought to ensure access to school in developing countries. But this focus has proved to be too limited; countries that have managed to increase their enrolment rates have frequently not seen the economic gains that were expected (Pritchett, 2006).

Three important conclusions can be drawn from the analysis of the knowledge capital of nations. First, low-income countries are even farther behind high-income countries than most people realised. There is virtually no overlap in learning in high- and low-income countries. Second, the problem of inclusion is not only faced by developing countries. High-income countries all have significant percentages of youth who do not have the basic skills required by the modern, information-based markets of the world. Third, many countries – usually poor countries – have never participated in international assessments, and for many of them, achievement would likely measure very low if they did. The available evidence that can be pieced together from regional tests generally supports this notion. On the other hand, the performance of Shanghai-China on PISA 2012 and of Mauritius on SACMEQ III does suggest some important heterogeneity among the countries that have not participated in the international tests.

NOTES

1. See, for example, the annual reports for the Education for All initiative, UNESCO (2014).

2. There have been previous attempts to catalogue available assessment data (e.g. Greaney and Kellaghan, 2008), but these have not combined different instruments and have not assessed basic skills. Filmer, Hasan and Pritchett (2006) use a PISA Level 1 standard and estimate values for those young people not in school for their sample of 11 countries that are intensively analysed.

3. TIMSS has broader coverage in the developing world. The 16 countries considered where achievement data come from TIMSS rather than PISA are Armenia, Bahrain, Botswana, Georgia, Ghana, Honduras, Iran, Lebanon, Macedonia, Morocco, Oman, Palestine, Saudi Arabia, South Africa, Syria and Ukraine.

4. The five countries with test-score information but without internationally comparable GDP data are Liechtenstein (average score 530 points; share below basic skills 0.137), Macao (529 points; 0.107), Palestine (388 points; 0.599), Shanghai-China (596 points; 0.036), and Syria (379 points; 0.646).

5. The GDP estimate is based on the purchasing-power-parity (PPP) share of the world total. Note that this is 58.6% of the world population outside China and India (which, by themselves, constitute 37.1% of the world population); see below for more on China and India.

6. Information on TERCE can be found in *Laboratorio Latinoamericano de Evaluación de la Calidad de la Educación* (2014). In other work, Hanushek and Woessmann (2012) linked the two earlier assessments (LLECE and SERCE) to the worldwide tests, allowing for a substantial expansion of the information on Latin America.

7. Honduras did not participate in PISA but did participate in TIMSS (although at ninth grade rather than the usually required eighth grade, thus with likely overstated performance). It is ranked 74 in the world rankings of 76 countries, and it is eclipsed in TERCE by Ecuador and Guatemala.

8. See Hungi et al. (2010) on SACMEQ. A second regional test in Africa (*Programme d'Analyse des Systèmes Éducatifs de la CONFEMEN*, or PASEC) provided achievement tests for a set of French-speaking countries, but there was no direct way to link these tests to the international testing.

9. Note that India participated in the First International Science Study (FISS) in 1971. Its combined score across the three age groups tested was 428, although this score was greatly affected by the score of 475 in the highly selected last year of school. It has not subsequently participated as a country in any of the international assessments.

10. Note that results for these two states are not included in the PISA 2009 report, but are available in the PISA online database.

11. *http://en.wikipedia.org/wiki/Indian_states_ranking_by_literacy_rate* [accessed February 24, 2015].

12. See *http://img.asercentre.org/docs/Publications/ASER%20Reports/ASER%202014/ fullaser2014mainreport_1.pdf* (accessed February 24, 2015).

13. See also the illustrations and the broader analysis of the ASER survey results in Pritchett (2013).

14. Results are reported separately for Hong Kong-China and Chinese Taipei (Taiwan), which have participated in testing and which enter into the growth analysis in Chapter 2 because of historically available economic data. Macao, which also participated, had scores of 538 points in mathematics and 521 points in science, which would place it eighth in the ranking, but it does not enter into the economic analysis.

15. For PISA participants, the enrolment rate is the total enrolled population of 15-year-olds at grade 7 or above divided by the total population of 15-year-olds. This is capped at 100% for three countries where it exceeds 100% due to differing data sources: Portugal 1.173, the United States 1.022, and the United Kingdom 1.010; see OECD (2013), Table A2.1. For TIMSS participants who did not participate in PISA, it is the net enrolment ratio in secondary education (as a percentage of the relevant group); see Mullis et al. (2012), based on World Development Indicators (WDI) 2011 and additional sources. Macedonia refers to the net enrolment ratio in 2005, the latest available from the WDI (where subsequent gross enrolment ratios indicate stability over time); Honduras refers to the gross enrolment ratio in 2011 from the WDI.

Notes regarding Cyprus

Readers should note the following information provided by Turkey and by the European Union Member States of the OECD and the European Union regarding the status of Cyprus:

Note by Turkey

The information in this document with reference to "Cyprus" relates to the southern part of the Island. There is no single authority representing both Turkish and Greek Cypriot people on the Island. Turkey recognises the Turkish Republic of Northern Cyprus (TRNC). Until a lasting and equitable solution is found within the context of the United Nations, Turkey shall preserve its position concerning the "Cyprus issue".

Note by all the European Union member States of the OECD and the European Union

The Republic of Cyprus is recognised by all members of the United Nations with the exception of Turkey. The information in this document relates to the area under the effective control of the Government of the Republic of Cyprus.

Note regarding Israel

The statistical data for Israel are supplied by and under the responsibility of the relevant Israeli authorities. The use of such data by the OECD is without prejudice to the status of the Golan Heights, East Jerusalem and Israeli settlements in the West Bank under the terms of international law.

REFERENCES

Das, J. and T. Zajonc (2010), "India shining and Bharat drowning: Comparing two Indian states to the worldwide distribution in mathematics achievement", *Journal of Development Economics*, Vol. 92/2, pp. 175-187.

Filmer, D., A. Hasan, and L.Pritchett (2006), "A millennium learning goal: Measuring real progress in education", *Working Paper*, No. 97, August, Center for Global Development, Washington, DC.

Greaney, V. and T. Kellaghan (2008), *Assessing National Achievement Levels in Education*, World Bank, Washington, DC.

Hanushek, E.A. and L.Woessmann (2012). "Schooling, educational achievement, and the Latin American growth puzzle", *Journal of Development Economics*, Vol. 99/2, pp. 497-512.

Hanushek, E.A. and L. Woessmann (2011), "Sample selectivity and the validity of international student achievement tests in economic research", *Economics Letters*, Vol. 110/2, pp. 79-82.

Hungi, N. et al. (2010), "SACMEQ III project results: Pupil achievement levels in reading and mathematics", Southern and Eastern Africa Consortium for Monitoring Educational Quality, Paris.

Laboratorio Latinoamericano de Evaluación de la Calidad de la Educación (2014), *Tercer Estudio Regional Comparativo y Explicativo (TERCE)*, Oficina Regional de Educación de la UNESCO para América Latina y el Caribe (OREALC/UNESCO), Santiago, Chile.

Mullis, I.V.S.et al (eds.) (2012), *TIMSS 2011 Encyclopedia: Education Policy and Curriculum in Mathematics and Science*, Vol. 1 and 2, TIMSS and PIRLS International Study Center, Boston College, Chestnut Hill, MA.

OECD (2013), *PISA 2012 Results: What Students Know and Can Do (Volume I, Revised edition, February 2014): Student Performance in Mathematics, Reading and Science*, OECD Publishing, Paris, http://dx.doi.org/10.1787/9789264208780-en.

Pritchett, L. (2013), *The Rebirth of Education: Schooling ain't Learning*, Center for Global Development, Washington, DC.

Pritchett, L. (2006), "Does learning to add up add up? The returns to schooling in aggregate data", in E.A. Hanushek and F. Welch (eds.), *Handbook of the Economics of Education*, North Holland, Amsterdam, pp. 635-695.

UNESCO (2014), *Teaching and Learning: Achieving Quality for All – Education For All Global Monitoring Report 2013/4*, United Nations Educational, Scientific and Cultural Organization (UNESCO), Paris.

Chapter 5

Economic impacts of achieving the basic skills goal by 2030

This chapter proposes three scenarios to examine the economic impact of achieving the goal of universal basic skills: each student now in school acquires a basic level of proficiency in mathematics and science; universal enrolment in secondary school, without changing the quality of schooling; and both universal enrolment and at least basic skills among all students. A fourth scenario posits improvements to be made over 30 years rather than over 15 years.

It is now possible to consider the proposed development goal – all youth acquire basic skills – in its relation to countries' access and achievement levels and to determine the economic value of achieving the goal. The idea is straightforward. For each of the 76 countries, the data show what kind of improvement would be necessary to reach the goal of universal basic skills. If the relationship between growth rates and achievement observed over the past half century holds into the future, one can calculate how much GDP would differ in the future if countries reached this development goal as opposed to doing nothing to change their knowledge capital. These projections allow both for the fact that education reform is not instantaneous (as implied by setting the goal to be achieved by 2030) and for the fact that the labour force changes as more skilled people progressively enter the labour market.

The analysis is decomposed into a series of reform projections that represent intermediate outcomes. The starting point is baseline projections in which achievement of students improves by 25 points in the Programme for International Student Assessment (PISA) test and in which gender achievement equalises for those now in school. The subsequent scenarios model reaching the goal of universal basic skills in separate steps: first, bringing all current students to basic skills (420 PISA points); second, achieving full participation in secondary school at current quality levels; and third, completely satisfying the goal by achieving full participation in school and bringing all students to basic skills.

These projections are followed by an analysis of the results' sensitivity to alterations in the estimation and projection approach. Finally, the report summarises and contrasts the alternative policy outcomes and shows unmistakably that improving schools so that all young people acquire basic skills should be the dominant objective.

Projection model and parameter choices

The projections rely on a simple description of how skills enter the labour market and have an impact on the economy.[1] The development goal is framed as the standard that should be met by 2030, leading to the assumption that improvement occurs linearly from today's schooling situation to attainment of the goal in 15 years. But of course, the labour force itself will only become more skilled as increasing numbers of new, better-trained people enter the labour market and replace the less-skilled individuals who retire. The analysis assumes that a worker remains in the labour force for 40 years, implying that the labour force will not be made up of fully skilled workers until 55 years have passed (15 years of reform and 40 years of replacing less-skilled workers as they retire).

The growth rate of the economy (according to the estimate of 1.98% higher annual growth rate per standard deviation in educational achievement; see column 3 of Table A.1 in Annex A) is calculated each year into the future based on the average skills of workers (which changes as new, more skilled workers enter). The gain in GDP is then estimated with an improved workforce over GDP with the existing workforce from 2015 until 2095.[2] The projection is carried out for 80 years to correspond to the life expectancy of somebody born in 2015.

Future gains in GDP are discounted to the present with a 3% discount rate. The resulting present value of additions to GDP is thus directly comparable to the current levels of GDP.[3] The gains to the discounted value of projected future GDP without reform can also be calculated to arrive at the average increase in total GDP over the 80 years.

Increasing average achievement of current students by 25 PISA points

In order to understand the impact of improved achievement, it is useful to begin with a simple improvement in existing schools equivalent to 25 PISA points. The improvement takes place by 2030 and involves no expansion in school enrolment. As discussed below, this kind of improvement is achievable by both low- and high-income countries. Some 28 countries have improved at this rate over the past 15 years.[4]

Table 5.1 summarises the results of this improvement for countries grouped by income category: lower-middle income countries, upper-middle income countries, high-income non-OECD countries, and high-income OECD countries. (The categories follow the World Bank classification of countries by income groups. No country classified as low income provides the international achievement data required for the projections.)

TABLE 5.1 EFFECT ON GDP OF INCREASING AVERAGE PERFORMANCE OF CURRENT STUDENTS BY 25 PISA POINTS

	Value of reform (bn USD)	In % of current GDP	In % of discounted future GDP	GDP increase in year 2095	Long-run growth increase	Increase in PISA score
Lower-middle income countries						
Armenia	75	293%	6.3%	25%	0.43	21.8
Georgia	99	271%	5.8%	23%	0.40	20.3
Ghana	175	150%	3.2%	13%	0.23	11.5
Honduras	100	246%	5.3%	21%	0.37	18.4
Indonesia	7 954	290%	6.2%	25%	0.43	21.6
Morocco	716	264%	5.6%	23%	0.39	19.8
Ukraine	1 095	285%	6.1%	25%	0.42	21.3
Viet Nam	1 149	210%	4.5%	18%	0.31	15.9
Upper-middle income countries						
Albania	70	216%	4.6%	19%	0.32	16.3
Argentina	2 926	315%	6.7%	27%	0.46	23.3
Botswana	70	198%	4.2%	17%	0.30	15.0
Brazil	8 256	260%	5.6%	23%	0.39	19.5
Bulgaria	366	286%	6.1%	25%	0.42	21.3
Colombia	1 580	231%	4.9%	20%	0.35	17.4
Costa Rica	198	264%	5.6%	23%	0.39	19.7
Hungary	825	330%	7.1%	29%	0.48	24.3
Iran	3 291	246%	5.3%	21%	0.37	18.5
Jordan	278	328%	7.0%	29%	0.48	24.2
Kazakhstan	1 450	323%	6.9%	28%	0.47	23.9
Lebanon	209	250%	5.3%	22%	0.37	18.8
Macedonia	75	259%	5.5%	22%	0.38	19.4
Malaysia	2 259	282%	6.0%	25%	0.42	21.0
Mexico	5 223	231%	4.9%	20%	0.34	17.4
Montenegro	34	340%	7.3%	30%	0.50	25.0
Peru	1 182	293%	6.3%	25%	0.43	21.8
Romania	1 371	340%	7.3%	30%	0.50	25.0
Serbia	299	320%	6.9%	28%	0.47	23.7
South Africa	1 703	239%	5.1%	21%	0.36	18.0
Thailand	2 820	267%	5.7%	23%	0.40	20.0
Tunisia	449	340%	7.3%	30%	0.50	25.0
Turkey	4 034	254%	5.4%	22%	0.38	19.1

TABLE 5.1 EFFECT ON GDP OF INCREASING AVERAGE PERFORMANCE OF CURRENT STUDENTS BY 25 PISA POINTS (continued)

	Value of reform (bn USD)	In % of current GDP	In % of discounted future GDP	GDP increase in year 2095	Long-run growth increase	Increase in PISA score
High-income non-OECD countries						
Bahrain	193	300%	6.4%	26%	0.44	22.3
Croatia	293	328%	7.0%	29%	0.48	24.2
Cyprus*	87	340%	7.3%	30%	0.50	25.0
Hong Kong-China	1 316	312%	6.7%	27%	0.46	23.1
Latvia	169	332%	7.1%	29%	0.48	24.5
Lithuania	259	312%	6.7%	27%	0.46	23.1
Oman	473	275%	5.9%	24%	0.41	20.5
Qatar	1 189	335%	7.2%	29%	0.49	24.7
Russian Federation	12 335	339%	7.2%	30%	0.49	24.9
Saudi Arabia	4 205	239%	5.1%	21%	0.36	18.0
Singapore	1 540	330%	7.1%	29%	0.48	24.3
Chinese Taipei	3 670	340%	7.3%	30%	0.49	25.0
United Arab Emirates	2 169	337%	7.2%	29%	0.49	24.8
Uruguay	208	285%	6.1%	25%	0.42	21.2
High-income OECD countries						
Australia	3 863	335%	7.2%	29%	0.49	24.7
Austria	1 293	322%	6.9%	28%	0.47	23.8
Belgium	1 611	334%	7.1%	29%	0.49	24.6
Canada	5 475	332%	7.1%	29%	0.49	24.5
Chile	1 341	310%	6.6%	27%	0.46	23.0
Czech Republic	1 019	326%	7.0%	28%	0.48	24.0
Denmark	857	332%	7.1%	29%	0.49	24.5
Estonia	123	334%	7.1%	29%	0.49	24.6
Finland	769	338%	7.2%	30%	0.49	24.9
France	8 575	322%	6.9%	28%	0.47	23.8
Germany	12 711	340%	7.3%	30%	0.50	25.0
Greece	959	322%	6.9%	28%	0.47	23.8
Iceland	49	339%	7.2%	30%	0.49	24.9
Ireland	782	332%	7.1%	29%	0.48	24.4
Israel*	905	322%	6.9%	28%	0.47	23.8
Italy	6 716	317%	6.8%	28%	0.46	23.4
Japan	16 311	332%	7.1%	29%	0.48	24.5
Korea	6 287	332%	7.1%	29%	0.48	24.5
Luxembourg	175	333%	7.1%	29%	0.49	24.6
Netherlands	2 788	338%	7.2%	30%	0.49	24.9
New Zealand	547	329%	7.0%	29%	0.48	24.3
Norway	1 194	339%	7.3%	30%	0.49	24.9
Poland	3 238	327%	7.0%	29%	0.48	24.1
Portugal	970	340%	7.3%	30%	0.50	25.0
Slovak Republic	529	338%	7.2%	30%	0.49	24.9
Slovenia	206	330%	7.1%	29%	0.48	24.3
Spain	5 134	323%	6.9%	28%	0.47	23.9
Sweden	1 542	339%	7.3%	30%	0.49	25.0
Switzerland	1 525	331%	7.1%	29%	0.48	24.4
United Kingdom	8 653	340%	7.3%	30%	0.50	25.0
United States	62 120	340%	7.3%	30%	0.50	25.0

* See notes at the end of this chapter.

Notes: Discounted value of future increases in GDP until 2095 due to the reform, expressed in billion dollars (PPP), as a percentage of current GDP, and as a percentage of discounted future GDP. "GDP increase in year 2095" indicates by how much GDP in 2095 is higher due to the reform (in %). "Long-run growth increase" refers to increase in annual growth rate (in percentage points) once the whole labour force has reached higher level of educational achievement. "Increase in PISA score" refers to the ultimate increase in educational achievement due to the reform. See text for reform parameters.

Note first that this improvement of 25 points would have a uniform effect on all countries if there were a 100% enrolment rate. The present value of added GDP would be 340% of a country's current GDP, or 7.3% higher GDP over the entire 80 years of the projection. By 2095, GDP would be 30% higher than that expected with today's skills level, representing the result of an annual growth rate that, in the end, is 0.5 percentage points higher. Of course, the total value of the added GDP differs by the size of the economy, so that the United States, for instance, would see a present value of gains of over USD 62 trillion, while much smaller Portugal would see gains of USD 970 billion.

Because enrolment is not fully universal, however, an increase of 25 points for those in school will have a varying (and lesser) impact on different countries.[5] Most of the high-income countries see close to these percentage gains because of their near-universal enrolment rates. The exceptions are the high-income countries that have historically relied on oil revenues and whose enrolment rates are comparatively low: Bahrain, Oman and Saudi Arabia. In the future, however, particularly if oil revenues become less significant, these countries will also have to rely on developing a skilled workforce in order to follow a sustainable development path. (Indeed, if oil revenues were to fall in the future because of supply reasons or changes in demand, the GDP of these oil countries might also fall, absent any skills improvement. The same would also hold for other resource-dependent economies if future revenues falter for some reason).

In most middle-income countries, where enrolment is more limited, merely improving the education of those currently in school has a more limited impact on the future labour force, and this shows up in economic gains. Albania, Botswana, Colombia, Ghana, Mexico and Viet Nam all see less than a 5% higher future GDP from this improvement. Yet history shows clearly that even for the countries with low enrolment rates, improving the quality of schools yields very large economic gains.

Obtaining the projected gains will require a variety of structural changes in each country's economy so that the new, more skilled workers can be productively absorbed into the labour force. However, these skill changes occur over a long period, giving firms in the different economies time to develop and adjust their production technologies. Such changes are simply a part of the productivity improvements seen over past half century.[6] Moreover, the record suggests that the technologies available when there is a more highly skilled workforce are superior in terms of productivity and output.

Achieving gender equality in achievement among current students

In seeking to achieve gender equality in schooling, development policy has focused almost exclusively on the issue of lower enrolment rates among girls. This report looks instead at achieving gender parity in learning.

Interestingly, in the 76 countries studied here, boys outperform girls (on average in mathematics and science) in 45 countries, whereas girls outperform boys in 31 countries.[7] The better-performing gender in each country is then used as an indicator of the achievement levels that are possible in the current schools.

For each country, the implications of a reform that lifts the lower-performing gender to the current average achievement of the higher-performing gender is then shown. Table 5.2 displays the results of this policy outcome.

TABLE 5.2 EFFECT ON GDP OF ATTAINING GENDER EQUALITY IN ACHIEVEMENT AMONG CURRENT STUDENTS

	Value of reform (bn USD)	In % of current GDP	In % of discounted future GDP	GDP increase in year 2095	Long-run growth increase	Increase in PISA score
Lower-middle income countries						
Armenia	21	83%	1.8%	7%	0.13	6.5
Georgia	8	22%	0.5%	2%	0.03	1.7
Ghana	90	77%	1.6%	6%	0.12	6.0
Honduras	48	118%	2.5%	10%	0.18	9.1
Indonesia	113	4%	0.1%	0%	0.01	0.3
Morocco	26	10%	0.2%	1%	0.02	0.8
Ukraine	79	21%	0.4%	2%	0.03	1.6
Viet Nam	129	24%	0.5%	2%	0.04	1.9
Upper-middle income countries						
Albania	5	17%	0.4%	1%	0.03	1.3
Argentina	201	22%	0.5%	2%	0.03	1.7
Botswana	17	46%	1.0%	4%	0.07	3.6
Brazil	1 597	50%	1.1%	4%	0.08	4.0
Bulgaria	82	64%	1.4%	5%	0.10	5.0
Colombia	699	102%	2.2%	9%	0.16	7.9
Costa Rica	72	95%	2.0%	8%	0.15	7.4
Hungary	98	39%	0.8%	3%	0.06	3.1
Iran	33	2%	0.1%	0%	0.00	0.2
Jordan	169	199%	4.3%	17%	0.30	15.1
Kazakhstan	109	24%	0.5%	2%	0.04	1.9
Lebanon	36	43%	0.9%	4%	0.07	3.4
Macedonia	19	65%	1.4%	5%	0.10	5.1
Malaysia	392	49%	1.0%	4%	0.08	3.8
Mexico	1 035	46%	1.0%	4%	0.07	3.6
Montenegro	5	53%	1.1%	4%	0.08	4.2
Peru	286	71%	1.5%	6%	0.11	5.5
Romania	16	4%	0.1%	0%	0.01	0.3
Serbia	14	15%	0.3%	1%	0.02	1.2
South Africa	180	25%	0.5%	2%	0.04	2.0
Thailand	781	74%	1.6%	6%	0.11	5.8
Tunisia	73	55%	1.2%	5%	0.09	4.3
Turkey	89	6%	0.1%	0%	0.01	0.4
High-income non-OECD countries						
Bahrain	206	320%	6.8%	28%	0.47	23.6
Croatia	25	28%	0.6%	2%	0.04	2.2
Cyprus*	10	40%	0.9%	3%	0.06	3.2
Hong Kong-China	253	60%	1.3%	5%	0.09	4.7
Latvia	31	61%	1.3%	5%	0.09	4.8
Lithuania	36	44%	0.9%	4%	0.07	3.4
Oman	691	401%	8.6%	35%	0.58	29.1
Qatar	600	169%	3.6%	14%	0.26	12.9
Russian Federation	813	22%	0.5%	2%	0.03	1.8

TABLE 5.2 EFFECT ON GDP OF ATTAINING GENDER EQUALITY IN ACHIEVEMENT AMONG CURRENT STUDENTS (continued)

	Value of reform (bn USD)	In % of current GDP	In % of discounted future GDP	GDP increase in year 2095	Long-run growth increase	Increase in PISA score
Saudi Arabia	1 780	101%	2.2%	9%	0.16	7.9
Singapore	57	12%	0.3%	1%	0.02	1.0
Chinese Taipei	218	20%	0.4%	2%	0.03	1.6
United Arab Emirates	661	103%	2.2%	9%	0.16	8.0
Uruguay	22	30%	0.6%	2%	0.05	2.3
High-income OECD countries						
Australia	594	52%	1.1%	4%	0.08	4.0
Austria	380	95%	2.0%	8%	0.15	7.4
Belgium	227	47%	1.0%	4%	0.07	3.7
Canada	664	40%	0.9%	3%	0.06	3.2
Chile	419	97%	2.1%	8%	0.15	7.5
Czech Republic	118	38%	0.8%	3%	0.06	3.0
Denmark	194	75%	1.6%	6%	0.12	5.9
Estonia	3	9%	0.2%	1%	0.01	0.7
Finland	143	63%	1.3%	5%	0.10	4.9
France	499	19%	0.4%	2%	0.03	1.5
Germany	1 523	41%	0.9%	3%	0.06	3.2
Greece	46	16%	0.3%	1%	0.02	1.2
Iceland	4	29%	0.6%	2%	0.05	2.3
Ireland	139	59%	1.3%	5%	0.09	4.6
Israel*	94	34%	0.7%	3%	0.05	2.6
Italy	1 298	61%	1.3%	5%	0.09	4.8
Japan	4 228	86%	1.8%	7%	0.13	6.7
Korea	1 180	62%	1.3%	5%	0.10	4.9
Luxembourg	66	126%	2.7%	11%	0.19	9.8
Netherlands	342	42%	0.9%	3%	0.06	3.3
New Zealand	99	59%	1.3%	5%	0.09	4.7
Norway	16	5%	0.1%	0%	0.01	0.4
Poland	40	4%	0.1%	0%	0.01	0.3
Portugal	85	30%	0.6%	2%	0.05	2.4
Slovak Republic	79	50%	1.1%	4%	0.08	4.0
Slovenia	11	17%	0.4%	1%	0.03	1.4
Spain	1 143	72%	1.5%	6%	0.11	5.6
Sweden	146	32%	0.7%	3%	0.05	2.5
Switzerland	270	59%	1.3%	5%	0.09	4.6
United Kingdom	2 100	82%	1.8%	7%	0.13	6.4
United States	1 614	9%	0.2%	1%	0.01	0.7

* See notes at the end of this chapter.

Notes: Discounted value of future increases in GDP until 2095 due to the reform, expressed in billion dollars (PPP), as a percentage of current GDP, and as a percentage of discounted future GDP. "GDP increase in year 2095" indicates by how much GDP in 2095 is higher due to the reform (in %). "Long-run growth increase" refers to increase in annual growth rate (in percentage points) once the whole labour force has reached higher level of educational achievement. "Increase in PISA score" refers to the ultimate increase in educational achievement due to the reform. See text for reform parameters.

The largest impacts on the economy – where the present value of GDP gains from growth is greater than 1.5 times current GDP – are found in Oman, Bahrain, Jordan and Qatar. In all of these countries, girls outperform boys, and the gains would come from increasing boys' skills.

It is important to remember that these results reflect data only for those enrolled in school. None of the improvement comes from change for those young people who are not in school. Moreover, a portion of the achievement gap might be explained by greater selection into schools for girls than boys. Unfortunately, neither this possibility nor the ramifications of any adjustments for differential enrolment can be easily explored, because the underlying data sources do not provide gender-specific enrolment rates.

The Education For All Global Monitoring Report for 2013/14 (UNESCO, 2014) reports a relatively low gender-parity index for gross enrolment rates in secondary schools for the Arab states, although it is slightly above that for sub-Saharan Africa and for South and West Asia. These values suggest the considerable untapped potential that would be released from closing gender achievement gaps coupled with a commensurate expansion in participation. Within this report, however, it is difficult to provide a precise quantitative evaluation of the components of this potential. The scenarios below, however, do so in the aggregate across genders without breaking out the gender effects explicitly.

Scenario I: Each current student attains a minimum of 420 PISA points

The following sections examine the goal of all youth reaching basic skill levels by 2030. Scenario I, which considers just those young people now in school, involves a somewhat artificial simulation whereby all students who score above 420 PISA points remain at their current level and only those who score under 420 points improve. In this scenario, all current students in each country acquire at least the basic skills. To estimate how this reform would improve the average achievement of each country, the performance of each student who now scores below 420 points is raised to 420 points and then the new average achievement of each country is calculated.[8]

Table 5.3 reports results on the impact of this policy. The heterogeneity of the impact is now even greater than considered in the previous sections, because the economic impact is driven by both the proportion of students in secondary school and their scores. Compare, for example, South Africa and Viet Nam. South Africa has the higher enrolment rate (72% vs. 64%), but the performance of students in Viet Nam is much higher than that of students in South Africa. As a result, this in-school policy increases South Africa's GDP over the next 80 years by almost 30%, on average, but it lifts GDP in Viet Nam by less than 1% because those currently in school achieve at the highest levels.

TABLE 5.3 EFFECT ON GDP OF EVERY CURRENT STUDENT ACQUIRING BASIC SKILLS

	Value of reform (bn USD)	In % of current GDP	In % of discounted future GDP	GDP increase in year 2095	Long-run growth increase	Increase in PISA score
Lower-middle income countries						
Armenia	110	429%	9.2%	38%	0.61	31.0
Georgia	212	579%	12.4%	52%	0.80	40.5
Ghana	1 101	944%	20.2%	90%	1.22	61.7
Honduras	468	1145%	24.5%	112%	1.43	72.2
Indonesia	18 569	677%	14.5%	62%	0.92	46.5
Morocco	2 747	1013%	21.7%	97%	1.29	65.4
Ukraine	748	195%	4.2%	17%	0.29	14.8
Viet Nam	209	38%	0.8%	3%	0.06	3.0
Upper-middle income countries						
Albania	147	455%	9.7%	41%	0.65	32.7
Argentina	5 632	605%	13.0%	55%	0.84	42.2
Botswana	190	533%	11.4%	48%	0.75	37.7
Brazil	14 823	467%	10.0%	42%	0.66	33.5
Bulgaria	434	339%	7.2%	30%	0.49	24.9
Colombia	3 310	485%	10.4%	43%	0.69	34.6
Costa Rica	231	308%	6.6%	27%	0.45	22.8
Hungary	417	167%	3.6%	14%	0.25	12.7
Iran	5 299	397%	8.5%	35%	0.57	28.8
Jordan	531	625%	13.4%	57%	0.86	43.4
Kazakhstan	1 449	323%	6.9%	28%	0.47	23.9
Lebanon	404	484%	10.3%	43%	0.68	34.5
Macedonia	202	697%	14.9%	64%	0.94	47.7
Malaysia	2 952	369%	7.9%	32%	0.53	27.0
Mexico	6 762	299%	6.4%	26%	0.44	22.2
Montenegro	55	553%	11.8%	50%	0.77	39.0
Peru	3 336	827%	17.7%	77%	1.09	55.2
Romania	1 194	296%	6.3%	26%	0.44	22.0
Serbia	280	299%	6.4%	26%	0.44	22.2
South Africa	9 782	1374%	29.4%	137%	1.65	83.4
Thailand	2 715	257%	5.5%	22%	0.38	19.3
Tunisia	903	683%	14.6%	63%	0.93	46.9
Turkey	2 968	187%	4.0%	16%	0.28	14.2
High-income non-OECD countries						
Bahrain	408	633%	13.5%	58%	0.87	43.9
Croatia	140	156%	3.3%	13%	0.24	12.0
Cyprus*						
Hong Kong-China	183	43%	0.9%	4%	0.07	3.4
Latvia	48	94%	2.0%	8%	0.14	7.3
Lithuania	114	138%	2.9%	12%	0.21	10.6
Oman	1 654	960%	20.5%	91%	1.24	62.5
Qatar	3 562	1005%	21.5%	96%	1.29	64.9
Russian Federation	5 303	146%	3.1%	12%	0.22	11.2

TABLE 5.3 EFFECT ON GDP OF EVERY CURRENT STUDENT ACQUIRING BASIC SKILLS (continued)

	Value of reform (bn USD)	In % of current GDP	In % of discounted future GDP	GDP increase in year 2095	Long-run growth increase	Increase in PISA score
Saudi Arabia	9 516	542%	11.6%	49%	0.76	38.2
Singapore	281	60%	1.3%	5%	0.09	4.7
Chinese Taipei	852	79%	1.7%	7%	0.12	6.1
United Arab Emirates	2 367	368%	7.9%	32%	0.53	26.9
Uruguay	355	486%	10.4%	43%	0.69	34.7
High-income OECD countries						
Australia	1 368	119%	2.5%	10%	0.18	9.2
Austria	459	114%	2.4%	10%	0.17	8.8
Belgium	729	151%	3.2%	13%	0.23	11.6
Canada	1 286	78%	1.7%	7%	0.12	6.1
Chile	1 405	325%	7.0%	28%	0.48	24.0
Czech Republic	381	122%	2.6%	10%	0.19	9.4
Denmark	302	117%	2.5%	10%	0.18	9.1
Estonia	14	39%	0.8%	3%	0.06	3.1
Finland	150	66%	1.4%	6%	0.10	5.1
France	4 415	166%	3.6%	14%	0.25	12.7
Germany	4 027	108%	2.3%	9%	0.17	8.3
Greece	724	243%	5.2%	21%	0.36	18.3
Iceland	28	193%	4.1%	17%	0.29	14.7
Ireland	216	92%	2.0%	8%	0.14	7.1
Israel*	847	301%	6.4%	26%	0.44	22.4
Italy	3 290	155%	3.3%	13%	0.24	11.9
Japan	3 256	66%	1.4%	6%	0.10	5.2
Korea	959	51%	1.1%	4%	0.08	4.0
Luxembourg	98	187%	4.0%	16%	0.28	14.2
Netherlands	777	94%	2.0%	8%	0.14	7.3
New Zealand	238	143%	3.1%	12%	0.22	11.0
Norway	588	167%	3.6%	14%	0.25	12.8
Poland	639	64%	1.4%	5%	0.10	5.0
Portugal	474	166%	3.6%	14%	0.25	12.7
Slovak Republic	387	247%	5.3%	21%	0.37	18.6
Slovenia	63	101%	2.2%	8%	0.15	7.8
Spain	2 156	136%	2.9%	12%	0.21	10.5
Sweden	930	205%	4.4%	18%	0.31	15.5
Switzerland	394	86%	1.8%	7%	0.13	6.7
United Kingdom	3 650	143%	3.1%	12%	0.22	11.0
United States	27 929	153%	3.3%	13%	0.23	11.7

* See notes at the end of this chapter.

Notes: Discounted value of future increases in GDP until 2095 due to the reform, expressed in billion dollars (PPP), as a percentage of current GDP, and as a percentage of discounted future GDP. "GDP increase in year 2095" indicates by how much GDP in 2095 is higher due to the reform (in %). "Long-run growth increase" refers to increase in annual growth rate (in percentage points) once the whole labour force has reached higher level of educational achievement. "Increase in PISA score" refers to the ultimate increase in educational achievement due to the reform. See text for reform parameters.

The present value of gains in a number of these countries is astounding. If current students in South Africa, Honduras, Morocco and Qatar were all to acquire basic skills, the gains would be over ten times the value of current GDP for those countries.

Figure 5.1 shows the distribution of increases in the present value of future GDP compared to current GDP levels by country. The high-income OECD countries – those that have historically been left out of discussions about goals for education improvement – have gains averaging 1.4 times their current GDP. This amounts to an average annual gain of 3% of future GDP over the next 80 years. The heterogeneity of the results reflects the variations in current performance across countries. While there is less than a 1.5% gain in Korea, Estonia, Singapore, Japan, Poland and Finland, the gain is over 6% in Israel. Again, gains for the high-income oil producers Qatar and Oman are very large: these countries would see a gain in GDP of more than 20% if all of their current students acquired basic skills.

FIGURE 5.1 EFFECT ON GDP OF EVERY CURRENT STUDENT ACQUIRING BASIC SKILLS (in % of current GDP)

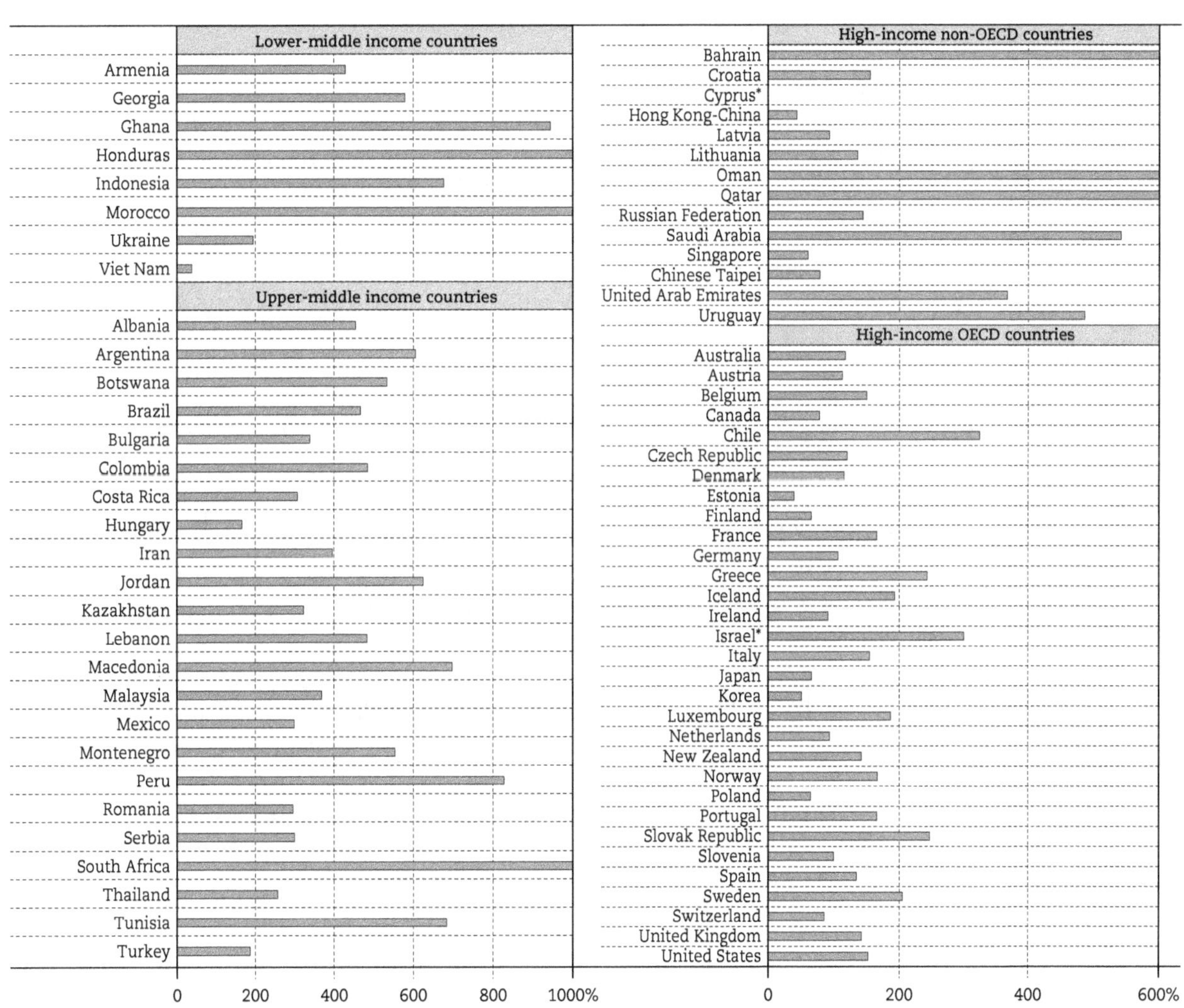

* See notes at the end of this chapter.

Notes: Discounted value of future increases in GDP until 2095 due to a reform that brings each student currently in school to a minimum of 420 PISA points, expressed as a percentage of current GDP. Value is 1 145% for Honduras, 1 013% for Morocco, 1 374% for South Africa, 960% for Oman and 1 005% for Qatar. See Table 5.3 for details.

Scenario II: Achieving full participation in secondary school at current quality

The estimates under Scenario I pertain to current schools and do not include any expansion of enrolment. For most of the high-income countries, enrolment expansion has little effect.[9] For most of the middle- and lower-income countries, however, access to education is an important component of economic improvement and has been central to much of the past policy discussion.

This section estimates the impact of providing all youth with access to schools at the current quality level (Scenario II). In the next section, the quality goal and the impact of full inclusion are jointly added to the analysis – i.e. all youth in the country acquire basic skills.

There is little information available about the skills level of young people not currently in school. Obviously, there are multiple reasons why young people are not enrolled, implying that youth outside of school have varying skills. For the projections, it is assumed that those currently not enrolled in school have an average achievement level equal to the 25th percentile of those currently in school in their country.[10] Of course, there is a lot of uncertainty about this assumption, which can serve only as a vague benchmark for any possible actual effect. For the calculations, young people who are not now enrolled in school do go to school, and they achieve at the average level of current students in the country. The achievement of those now in school does not change.[11] Countries like Brazil and Mexico, which have raised enrolment rates significantly over the past decade without lowering achievement levels, do show that this is possible.

Table 5.4 shows the estimates of how each country's current system would expand under Scenario II. These estimates, following in the spirit of the prior Education for All and Millennium Development Goals, identify the lost economic opportunities from limited access to schools.

The size of the loss is obviously related to how far a country is from universal enrolment, but it is also affected by the variation in quality of students. Figure 5.2 shows the present value of GDP gains over the current GDP of each country under Scenario II. For the high-income OECD countries, the gains average 19% and are uniformly below one-half of current GDP (except for Italy and Chile). But in the high-income non-OECD countries, 4 out of the 14 countries (Saudi Arabia, Oman, Uruguay and Bahrain) would see gains that exceed their current GDP.

Of course the largest gains come in the middle-income countries. Nine countries would gain more than double their current GDP from simple expansion at the current quality levels.[12] Note again that Viet Nam, a high-achieving country on the PISA rankings, would gain dramatically by expanding its system – if it is also able to maintain the current quality of its schools.

The difficulty with a policy of expanded enrolment – one seen repeatedly over the past decades as the policy has been implemented – is that countries may focus on access without clear commitment to quality. Many of the policies designed to promote broader enrolment, such as conditional cash transfers or various enrolment subsidies, have brought more students into the classroom, but they have failed to improve education outcomes.[13] These estimates of expansion at current quality levels are provided in order to show how attaining basic skills adds value, even if mere expansion should not be considered an effective policy goal.

TABLE 5.4 EFFECT ON GDP OF UNIVERSAL ENROLMENT IN SECONDARY SCHOOL AT CURRENT SCHOOL QUALITY

	Value of reform (bn USD)	In % of current GDP	In % of discounted future GDP	GDP increase in year 2095	Long-run growth increase	Increase in PISA score
Lower-middle income countries						
Armenia	28	109%	2.3%	9%	0.17	8.4
Georgia	62	169%	3.6%	14%	0.26	12.9
Ghana	644	552%	11.8%	50%	0.77	38.9
Honduras	78	191%	4.1%	16%	0.29	14.5
Indonesia	2 292	84%	1.8%	7%	0.13	6.5
Morocco	455	168%	3.6%	14%	0.25	12.8
Ukraine	425	111%	2.4%	9%	0.17	8.6
Viet Nam	1 431	261%	5.6%	23%	0.39	19.6
Upper-middle income countries						
Albania	85	265%	5.7%	23%	0.39	19.8
Argentina	438	47%	1.0%	4%	0.07	3.7
Botswana	120	336%	7.2%	29%	0.49	24.7
Brazil	5 220	165%	3.5%	14%	0.25	12.6
Bulgaria	173	135%	2.9%	11%	0.21	10.4
Colombia	1 392	204%	4.4%	17%	0.31	15.4
Costa Rica	97	128%	2.7%	11%	0.20	9.9
Hungary	53	21%	0.5%	2%	0.03	1.7
Iran	3 054	229%	4.9%	20%	0.34	17.2
Jordan	18	21%	0.5%	2%	0.03	1.7
Kazakhstan	127	28%	0.6%	2%	0.04	2.2
Lebanon	175	209%	4.5%	18%	0.31	15.8
Macedonia	69	237%	5.1%	20%	0.35	17.9
Malaysia	924	115%	2.5%	10%	0.18	8.9
Mexico	4 403	195%	4.2%	17%	0.29	14.8
Montenegro	0	0%	0.0%	0%	0.00	0.0
Peru	368	91%	2.0%	8%	0.14	7.1
Romania	0	0%	0.0%	0%	0.00	0.0
Serbia	38	41%	0.9%	3%	0.06	3.2
South Africa	1 929	271%	5.8%	23%	0.40	20.2
Thailand	1 472	140%	3.0%	12%	0.21	10.7
Tunisia	0	0%	0.0%	0%	0.00	0.0
Turkey	3 045	192%	4.1%	16%	0.29	14.6
High-income non-OECD countries						
Bahrain	65	101%	2.2%	9%	0.16	7.9
Croatia	23	26%	0.6%	2%	0.04	2.0
Cyprus*	0	0%	0.0%	0%	0.00	0.0
Hong Kong-China	227	54%	1.2%	5%	0.08	4.2
Latvia	8	15%	0.3%	1%	0.02	1.2
Lithuania	48	58%	1.2%	5%	0.09	4.5
Oman	320	186%	4.0%	16%	0.28	14.1
Qatar	37	11%	0.2%	1%	0.02	0.8
Russian Federation	81	2%	0.0%	0%	0.00	0.2
Saudi Arabia	3 997	227%	4.9%	20%	0.34	17.2
Singapore	117	25%	0.5%	2%	0.04	2.0
Chinese Taipei	1	0%	0.0%	0%	0.00	0.0
United Arab Emirates	41	6%	0.1%	1%	0.01	0.5
Uruguay	89	122%	2.6%	10%	0.19	9.4

TABLE 5.4 EFFECT ON GDP OF UNIVERSAL ENROLMENT IN SECONDARY SCHOOL AT CURRENT SCHOOL QUALITY (continued)

	Value of reform (bn USD)	In % of current GDP	In % of discounted future GDP	GDP increase in year 2095	Long-run growth increase	Increase in PISA score
High-income OECD countries						
Australia	128	11%	0.2%	1%	0.02	0.9
Austria	157	39%	0.8%	3%	0.06	3.1
Belgium	67	14%	0.3%	1%	0.02	1.1
Canada	251	15%	0.3%	1%	0.02	1.2
Chile	253	59%	1.3%	5%	0.09	4.6
Czech Republic	97	31%	0.7%	3%	0.05	2.4
Denmark	38	15%	0.3%	1%	0.02	1.2
Estonia	4	12%	0.2%	1%	0.02	0.9
Finland	9	4%	0.1%	0%	0.01	0.3
France	1 055	40%	0.8%	3%	0.06	3.1
Germany	0	0%	0.0%	0%	0.00	0.0
Greece	111	37%	0.8%	3%	0.06	2.9
Iceland	0	2%	0.1%	0%	0.00	0.2
Ireland	38	16%	0.3%	1%	0.03	1.3
Israel*	126	45%	1.0%	4%	0.07	3.5
Italy	1 094	52%	1.1%	4%	0.08	4.0
Japan	843	17%	0.4%	1%	0.03	1.4
Korea	315	17%	0.4%	1%	0.03	1.3
Luxembourg	8	15%	0.3%	1%	0.02	1.2
Netherlands	28	3%	0.1%	0%	0.01	0.3
New Zealand	45	27%	0.6%	2%	0.04	2.1
Norway	6	2%	0.0%	0%	0.00	0.1
Poland	269	27%	0.6%	2%	0.04	2.1
Portugal	0	0%	0.0%	0%	0.00	0.0
Slovak Republic	8	5%	0.1%	0%	0.01	0.4
Slovenia	14	23%	0.5%	2%	0.04	1.8
Spain	531	33%	0.7%	3%	0.05	2.6
Sweden	2	0%	0.0%	0%	0.00	0.0
Switzerland	82	18%	0.4%	1%	0.03	1.4
United Kingdom	0	0%	0.0%	0%	0.00	0.0
United States	0	0%	0.0%	0%	0.00	0.0

* See notes at the end of this chapter.

Notes: Discounted value of future increases in GDP until 2095 due to the reform, expressed in billion dollars (PPP), as a percentage of current GDP, and as a percentage of discounted future GDP. "GDP increase in year 2095" indicates by how much GDP in 2095 is higher due to the reform (in %). "Long-run growth increase" refers to increase in annual growth rate (in percentage points) once the whole labour force has reached higher level of educational achievement. "Increase in PISA score" refers to the ultimate increase in educational achievement due to the reform. See text for reform parameters.

FIGURE 5.2 EFFECT ON GDP OF UNIVERSAL ENROLMENT IN SECONDARY SCHOOL AT CURRENT SCHOOL QUALITY (in % of current GDP)

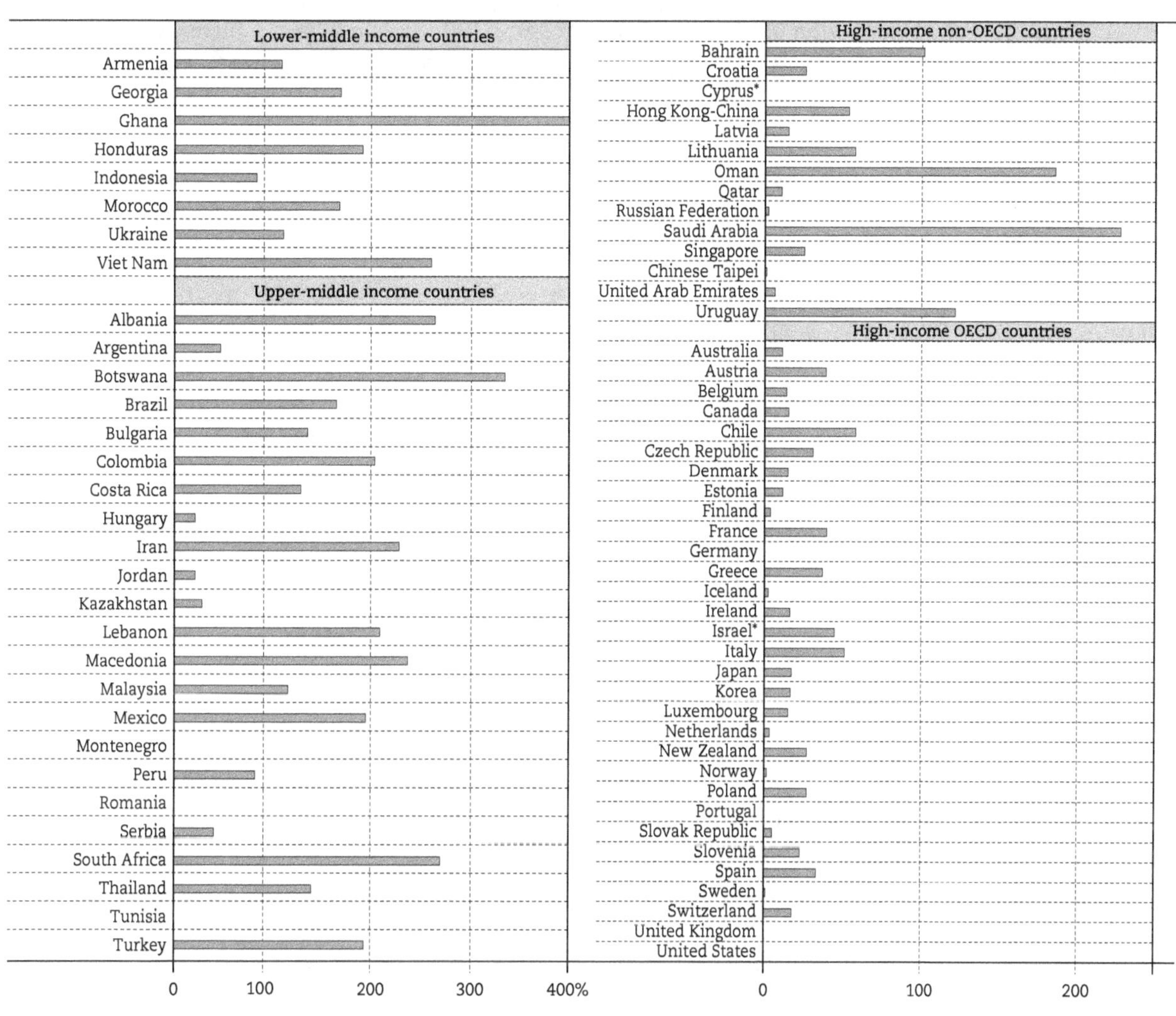

* See notes at the end of this chapter.

Notes: Discounted value of future increases in GDP until 2095 due to a reform that achieves full participation in secondary school at current quality, expressed as a percentage of current GDP. Value is 552% for Ghana. See Table 5.4 for details.

Scenario III: Achieving full participation in secondary school and every student attains a minimum of 420 PISA points

The implications of meeting the proposed development goal of all youth reaching basic skill levels by 2030 can now be considered. This goal combines universal access with quality improvement and has meaning for all countries. The performance of those young people currently not in school is raised either to the mean achievement of the country's current students or to 420 points, whichever is higher.

Table 5.5 presents the projected gains for each country under this third scenario. Unsurprisingly, the lowest-income countries of the sample would show by far the largest gains. The simple estimates for the eight lower-middle income countries indicate a present value of gains averaging 13 times the current GDP of these countries. Translated into a percentage of future GDP, this implies a GDP that is 28% higher, on average, every year for the next 80 years. By the end of the projection period in 2095, GDP with school improvement would average some 140% greater than would be expected with the current skills of the labour force.

TABLE 5.5 EFFECT ON GDP OF UNIVERSAL ENROLMENT IN SECONDARY SCHOOL AND EVERY STUDENT ACQUIRING BASIC SKILLS

	Value of reform (bn USD)	In % of current GDP	In % of discounted future GDP	GDP increase in year 2095	Long-run growth increase	Increase in PISA score
Lower-middle income countries						
Armenia	143	561%	12.0%	51%	0.78	39.4
Georgia	315	858%	18.4%	81%	1.13	57.0
Ghana	4 526	3 881%	83.0%	477%	3.37	170.3
Honduras	824	2 016%	43.1%	215%	2.20	111.0
Indonesia	24 409	889%	19.0%	84%	1.16	58.7
Morocco	4 316	1 591%	34.0%	163%	1.85	93.3
Ukraine	1 213	316%	6.8%	28%	0.46	23.4
Viet Nam	1 667	304%	6.5%	26%	0.45	22.6
Upper-middle income countries						
Albania	300	929%	19.9%	88%	1.21	60.9
Argentina	6 448	693%	14.8%	64%	0.94	47.5
Botswana	465	1 303%	27.9%	129%	1.58	80.0
Brazil	23 841	751%	16.1%	70%	1.01	50.9
Bulgaria	636	496%	10.6%	44%	0.70	35.4
Colombia	6 218	910%	19.5%	86%	1.19	59.9
Costa Rica	346	461%	9.9%	41%	0.65	33.1
Hungary	474	190%	4.1%	16%	0.29	14.4
Iran	8 946	670%	14.3%	61%	0.91	46.1
Jordan	565	665%	14.2%	61%	0.91	45.8
Kazakhstan	1 596	356%	7.6%	31%	0.52	26.1
Lebanon	682	816%	17.5%	76%	1.08	54.6
Macedonia	329	1 137%	24.3%	111%	1.42	71.8
Malaysia	4 043	505%	10.8%	45%	0.71	35.9
Mexico	12 448	551%	11.8%	50%	0.77	38.8
Montenegro	55	553%	11.8%	50%	0.77	39.0
Peru	4 341	1 076%	23.0%	104%	1.36	68.7
Romania	1 194	296%	6.3%	26%	0.44	22.0
Serbia	323	346%	7.4%	30%	0.50	25.5
South Africa	18 678	2 624%	56.1%	295%	2.63	133.1
Thailand	4 371	414%	8.9%	37%	0.59	30.0
Tunisia	903	683%	14.6%	63%	0.93	46.9
Turkey	6 288	396%	8.5%	35%	0.57	28.8
High-income non-OECD countries						
Bahrain	510	789%	16.9%	74%	1.05	53.1
Croatia	164	184%	3.9%	16%	0.28	14.0
Cyprus*						
Hong Kong-China	414	98%	2.1%	8%	0.15	7.6
Latvia	56	109%	2.3%	9%	0.17	8.5
Lithuania	166	200%	4.3%	17%	0.30	15.1
Oman	2 459	1 427%	30.5%	143%	1.70	85.9
Qatar	3 649	1 029%	22.0%	99%	1.31	66.2

TABLE 5.5 EFFECT ON GDP OF UNIVERSAL ENROLMENT IN SECONDARY SCHOOL AND EVERY STUDENT ACQUIRING BASIC SKILLS (continued)

	Value of reform (bn USD)	In % of current GDP	In % of discounted future GDP	GDP increase in year 2095	Long-run growth increase	Increase in PISA score
Russian Federation	5 389	148%	3.2%	13%	0.22	11.4
Saudi Arabia	17 134	975%	20.9%	93%	1.25	63.4
Singapore	402	86%	1.8%	7%	0.13	6.7
Chinese Taipei	852	79%	1.7%	7%	0.12	6.2
United Arab Emirates	2 415	375%	8.0%	33%	0.54	27.4
Uruguay	479	656%	14.0%	60%	0.90	45.2
High-income OECD countries						
Australia	1 504	130%	2.8%	11%	0.20	10.1
Austria	624	156%	3.3%	13%	0.24	11.9
Belgium	801	166%	3.6%	14%	0.25	12.7
Canada	1 546	94%	2.0%	8%	0.14	7.3
Chile	1 698	393%	8.4%	35%	0.57	28.6
Czech Republic	483	154%	3.3%	13%	0.23	11.8
Denmark	342	133%	2.8%	11%	0.20	10.2
Estonia	19	51%	1.1%	4%	0.08	4.0
Finland	159	70%	1.5%	6%	0.11	5.4
France	5 554	209%	4.5%	18%	0.31	15.8
Germany	4 027	108%	2.3%	9%	0.17	8.3
Greece	848	285%	6.1%	25%	0.42	21.2
Iceland	28	196%	4.2%	17%	0.29	14.9
Ireland	257	109%	2.3%	9%	0.17	8.4
Israel*	991	353%	7.6%	31%	0.51	25.9
Italy	4 466	210%	4.5%	18%	0.32	15.9
Japan	4 126	84%	1.8%	7%	0.13	6.5
Korea	1 282	68%	1.4%	6%	0.10	5.3
Luxembourg	107	204%	4.4%	17%	0.31	15.4
Netherlands	806	98%	2.1%	8%	0.15	7.6
New Zealand	286	172%	3.7%	15%	0.26	13.1
Norway	595	169%	3.6%	14%	0.26	12.9
Poland	916	92%	2.0%	8%	0.14	7.2
Portugal	474	166%	3.6%	14%	0.25	12.7
Slovak Republic	396	253%	5.4%	22%	0.38	19.0
Slovenia	78	124%	2.7%	11%	0.19	9.6
Spain	2 721	171%	3.7%	15%	0.26	13.1
Sweden	933	205%	4.4%	18%	0.31	15.6
Switzerland	479	104%	2.2%	9%	0.16	8.1
United Kingdom	3 650	143%	3.1%	12%	0.22	11.0
United States	27 929	153%	3.3%	13%	0.23	11.7

* See notes at the end of this chapter.

Notes: Discounted value of future increases in GDP until 2095 due to the reform, expressed in billion dollars (PPP), as a percentage of current GDP, and as a percentage of discounted future GDP. "GDP increase in year 2095" indicates by how much GDP in 2095 is higher due to the reform (in %). "Long-run growth increase" refers to increase in annual growth rate (in percentage points) once the whole labour force has reached higher level of educational achievement. "Increase in PISA score" refers to the ultimate increase in educational achievement due to the reform. See text for reform parameters.

Increases of this magnitude are, of course, unlikely, because the gains in achievement over the next 15 years are outside any real expectations. Ghana and Honduras, for example, would require an increase in achievement of over one standard deviation during this period. Nothing like that has ever been seen. But the calculations do show the value of improvement and suggest the lengths to which a country should be willing to go to improve its schools.

Figure 5.3 compares the gains from attaining universal basic skills (in present value terms) to current GDP. Perhaps the most interesting part of the figure is the right side. It shows that among the high-income non-OECD countries, the impact on the oil-producing countries is particularly dramatic. Improved basic skills among the populations of Oman, Qatar and Saudi Arabia imply gains exceeding eight times current GDP for these countries, and Bahrain follows closely. If oil resources are depleted or if the price of oil falls, say through new technologies, these countries will have to rely on the skills of their populations – and the data suggest there is substantial room for improvement.

FIGURE 5.3 EFFECT ON GDP OF UNIVERSAL ENROLMENT IN SECONDARY SCHOOL AND EVERY STUDENT ACQUIRING BASIC SKILLS (in % of current GDP)

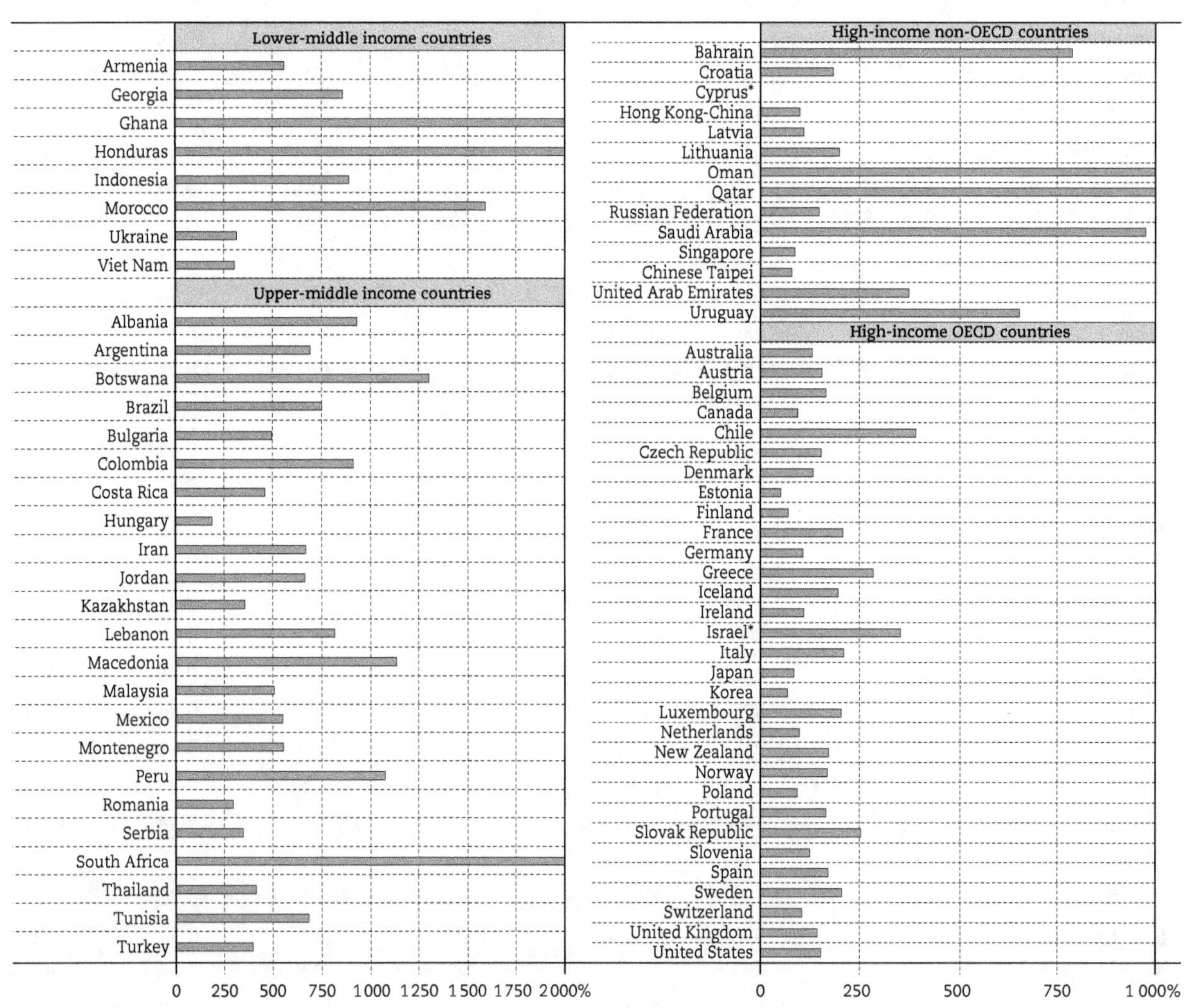

* See notes at the end of this chapter.

Notes: Discounted value of future increases in GDP until 2095 due to a reform that achieves full participation in secondary school and brings each student to a minimum of 420 PISA points, expressed as a percentage of current GDP. Value is 3 881% for Ghana, 2 016% for Honduras, 2 624% for South Africa, 1 427% for Oman and 1 029% for Qatar. See Table 5.5 for details.

Equally interesting are the high-income OECD countries, which typically do not figure in discussions of development goals. For 8 of these 31 countries, the present value of GDP gains from meeting the basic skills goal would be more than twice the size of their current GDP.[14] The average gain across the high-income OECD countries is 162% of current GDP. This implies a GDP that is on average 3.5% higher than would be expected with no improvement in the quality of the schools (see Figure 5.4). Almost all of the gain comes from improving achievement at the bottom end, since enrolment in these countries is near universal.[15]

FIGURE 5.4 EFFECT ON GDP OF UNIVERSAL ENROLMENT IN SECONDARY SCHOOL AND EVERY STUDENT ACQUIRING BASIC SKILLS (in % of discounted future GDP)

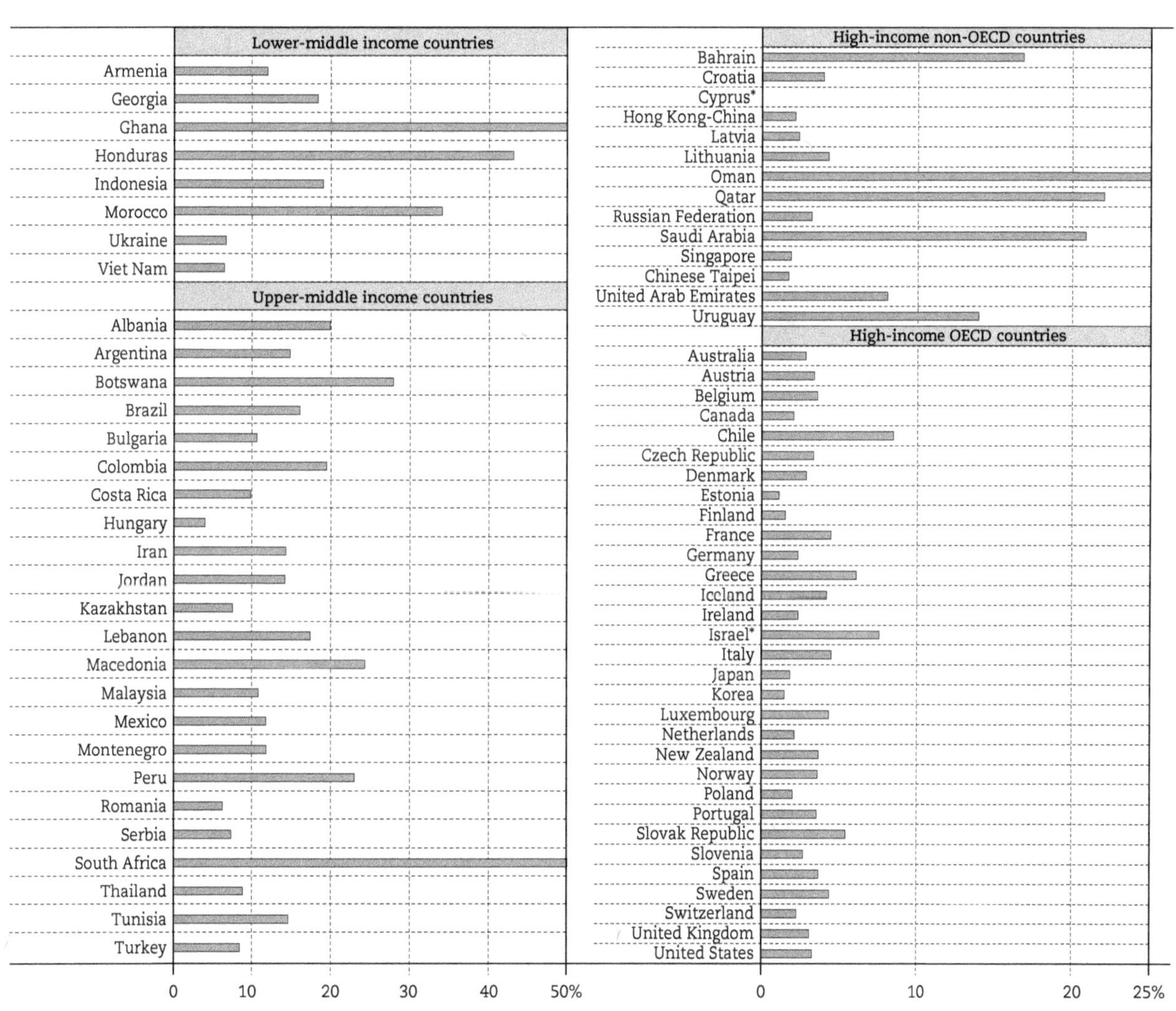

* See notes at the end of this chapter.

Notes: Discounted value of future increases in GDP until 2095 due to a reform that achieves full participation in secondary school and brings each student to a minimum of 420 PISA points, expressed as a percentage of discounted future GDP. Value is 83.0% for Ghana, 56.1% for South Africa and 30.5% for Oman. See Table 5.5 for details.

Scenario IV: Scenario III with 30-year improvement

Changing the quality of schools takes time. Changing the teaching force, for example, frequently means attracting a new group of people into teaching, altering their training, establishing new pay and incentive structures, and waiting for retirements so that the new teachers can be hired. Moreover, the full benefit of the new teaching staff is obtained only after students experience an entire education career with the new teachers. Moving to universal access also takes time because it involves adding both new personnel and new facilities. For all these reasons, the desired gains in achievement are likely to come slowly.

Here, the impact of a fourth scenario is considered, which lengthens the period before universal basic skills are attained. The prior estimates of economic gains all relied on quality improvements taking place by 2030 – that is, in 15 years – rather than the 30 years considered here. Relatively quickly-met goals might be more politically feasible in the sense that tangible gains could be seen sooner, but they might also be unrealistic.

The estimates for the last scenario, in which the goal of universal basic skills was met, are now reproduced, except that 30 years rather than 15 years are allowed to carry out the improvements. Two facets of this estimation, which is shown in Table 5.6, stand out. First, fairly obviously, the pattern of gains across countries remains the same as that seen in Table 5.5. Second, while the lengthened time frame under Scenario IV reduces the magnitude of economic gain, the gains remain stunningly large. For example, among the lower-middle income countries, the average gain is "only" a bit over nine times current GDP, as compared with 13 times under the 15-year calculations in Scenario III.

TABLE 5.6 **EFFECT ON GDP OF UNIVERSAL ENROLMENT IN SECONDARY SCHOOL AND EVERY STUDENT ACQUIRING BASIC SKILLS, ACHIEVED OVER 30 YEARS**

	Value of reform (bn USD)	In % of current GDP	In % of discounted future GDP	GDP increase in year 2095	Long-run growth increase	Increase in PISA score
Lower-middle income countries						
Armenia	106	414%	8.9%	42%	0.78	39.4
Georgia	230	628%	13.4%	66%	1.13	57.0
Ghana	3 077	2 638%	56.4%	352%	3.37	170.3
Honduras	584	1 428%	30.5%	168%	2.20	111.0
Indonesia	17 837	650%	13.9%	69%	1.16	58.7
Morocco	3 091	1 139%	24.4%	130%	1.85	93.3
Ukraine	903	235%	5.0%	23%	0.46	23.4
Viet Nam	1 242	227%	4.8%	22%	0.45	22.6
Upper-middle income countries						
Albania	219	678%	14.5%	72%	1.21	60.9
Argentina	4 741	510%	10.9%	53%	0.94	47.5
Botswana	335	940%	20.1%	104%	1.58	80.0
Brazil	17 497	551%	11.8%	58%	1.01	50.9
Bulgaria	470	367%	7.9%	37%	0.70	35.4
Colombia	4 541	665%	14.2%	71%	1.19	59.9
Costa Rica	257	342%	7.3%	34%	0.65	33.1
Hungary	355	142%	3.0%	14%	0.29	14.4
Iran	6 583	493%	10.5%	51%	0.91	46.1
Jordan	415	489%	10.5%	51%	0.91	45.8
Kazakhstan	1 187	265%	5.7%	26%	0.52	26.1
Lebanon	499	597%	12.8%	63%	1.08	54.6
Macedonia	238	824%	17.6%	90%	1.42	71.8

TABLE 5.6 EFFECT ON GDP OF UNIVERSAL ENROLMENT IN SECONDARY SCHOOL AND EVERY STUDENT ACQUIRING BASIC SKILLS, ACHIEVED OVER 30 YEARS (continued)

	Value of reform (bn USD)	In % of current GDP	In % of discounted future GDP	GDP increase in year 2095	Long-run growth increase	Increase in PISA score
Malaysia	2 991	374%	8.0%	38%	0.71	35.9
Mexico	9 196	407%	8.7%	41%	0.77	38.8
Montenegro	41	409%	8.7%	42%	0.77	39.0
Peru	3 154	782%	16.7%	85%	1.36	68.7
Romania	890	221%	4.7%	22%	0.44	22.0
Serbia	241	258%	5.5%	26%	0.50	25.5
South Africa	13 035	1 831%	39.2%	226%	2.63	133.1
Thailand	3 244	307%	6.6%	31%	0.59	30.0
Tunisia	664	503%	10.8%	52%	0.93	46.9
Turkey	4 669	294%	6.3%	29%	0.57	28.8
High-income non-OECD countries						
Bahrain	374	579%	12.4%	61%	1.05	53.1
Croatia	123	138%	2.9%	13%	0.28	14.0
Cyprus*						
Hong Kong-China	311	74%	1.6%	7%	0.15	7.6
Latvia	42	82%	1.8%	8%	0.17	8.5
Lithuania	124	149%	3.2%	15%	0.30	15.1
Oman	1 769	1 026%	22.0%	115%	1.70	85.9
Qatar	2 655	749%	16.0%	81%	1.31	66.2
Russian Federation	4 037	111%	2.4%	11%	0.22	11.4
Saudi Arabia	12 488	711%	15.2%	76%	1.25	63.4
Singapore	302	65%	1.4%	6%	0.13	6.7
Chinese Taipei	640	59%	1.3%	6%	0.12	6.2
United Arab Emirates	1 794	279%	6.0%	28%	0.54	27.4
Uruguay	353	483%	10.3%	50%	0.90	45.2
High-income OECD countries						
Australia	1 127	98%	2.1%	9%	0.20	10.1
Austria	468	117%	2.5%	11%	0.24	11.9
Belgium	600	124%	2.7%	12%	0.25	12.7
Canada	1 161	70%	1.5%	7%	0.14	7.3
Chile	1 261	292%	6.2%	29%	0.57	28.6
Czech Republic	362	116%	2.5%	11%	0.23	11.8
Denmark	256	99%	2.1%	10%	0.20	10.2
Estonia	14	38%	0.8%	4%	0.08	4.0
Finland	119	52%	1.1%	5%	0.11	5.4
France	4 151	156%	3.3%	15%	0.31	15.8
Germany	3 021	81%	1.7%	8%	0.17	8.3
Greece	632	212%	4.5%	21%	0.42	21.2
Iceland	21	146%	3.1%	14%	0.29	14.9
Ireland	193	82%	1.7%	8%	0.17	8.4
Israel*	737	262%	5.6%	26%	0.51	25.9
Italy	3 338	157%	3.4%	15%	0.32	15.9
Japan	3 098	63%	1.3%	6%	0.13	6.5
Korea	963	51%	1.1%	5%	0.10	5.3
Luxembourg	80	152%	3.3%	15%	0.31	15.4
Netherlands	605	73%	1.6%	7%	0.15	7.6
New Zealand	214	129%	2.8%	12%	0.26	13.1

TABLE 5.6 EFFECT ON GDP OF UNIVERSAL ENROLMENT IN SECONDARY SCHOOL AND EVERY STUDENT ACQUIRING BASIC SKILLS, ACHIEVED OVER 30 YEARS (continued)

	Value of reform (bn USD)	In % of current GDP	In % of discounted future GDP	GDP increase in year 2095	Long-run growth increase	Increase in PISA score
Norway	445	126%	2.7%	12%	0.26	12.9
Poland	687	69%	1.5%	7%	0.14	7.2
Portugal	355	124%	2.7%	12%	0.25	12.7
Slovak Republic	296	189%	4.0%	19%	0.38	19.0
Slovenia	58	93%	2.0%	9%	0.19	9.6
Spain	2 037	128%	2.7%	12%	0.26	13.1
Sweden	697	153%	3.3%	15%	0.31	15.6
Switzerland	360	78%	1.7%	8%	0.16	8.1
United Kingdom	2 735	107%	2.3%	10%	0.22	11.0
United States	20 917	114%	2.4%	11%	0.23	11.7

* See notes at the end of this chapter.

Notes: Discounted value of future increases in GDP until 2095 due to the reform, expressed in billion dollars (PPP), as a percentage of current GDP, and as a percentage of discounted future GDP. "GDP increase in year 2095" indicates by how much GDP in 2095 is higher due to the reform (in %). "Long-run growth increase" refers to increase in annual growth rate (in percentage points) once the whole labour force has reached higher level of educational achievement. "Increase in PISA score" refers to the ultimate increase in educational achievement due to the reform. See text for reform parameters.

Robustness of projections

The projections described in the various scenarios above rely upon a common model of growth and a common set of economic parameters. It is useful to see how altering these projections affects the results. Two major alterations to the original analysis are considered: including a "neoclassical growth model", where education makes labour and capital more efficient but does not change growth rates in the long run; and including institutional measures related to the quality of the underlying economic environment.[16]

NEOCLASSICAL GROWTH

The projections so far assume that higher educational achievement allows a country to keep on growing at a higher rate in the long run. Such a specification captures the basic ideas of what economists call endogenous growth theory, where a better-educated workforce leads to a larger stream of new ideas that produces technological progress at a higher rate. In the contrasting augmented neoclassical growth model, changes in test scores lead to higher steady-state levels of income but do not affect the long-run growth path. An alternative approach for the projections is thus to interpret the growth model in the neoclassical rather than endogenous-growth framework.[17] The neoclassical model converges to a 1.5% growth rate in the steady state, and this implies slower growth than would be predicted by the increased knowledge capital under the universal acquisition of basic skills, thus lowering the total estimated gains.

For purposes of comparison, the basic growth model is re-estimated and projections are performed based on the neoclassical model.[18] Table 5.7 provides a direct comparison across country income groups of meeting the goal of universal basic skills by 2030 (Scenario III) using the two sets of estimates, one with the endogenous growth model and one with the neoclassical growth model. Country-by-country results of the neoclassical projection model for all scenarios are found in Table C.1 in Annex C.

TABLE 5.7 COMPARISON OF ESTIMATES WITH ENDOGENOUS AND AUGMENTED NEOCLASSICAL GROWTH MODELS

	Endogenous growth model		Augmented neoclassical model	
	In % of current GDP	In % of discounted future GDP	In % of current GDP	In % of discounted future GDP
Lower-middle income countries	1 302%	27.9%	679%	18.0%
Upper-middle income countries	731%	15.6%	383%	10.7%
High-income non-OECD countries	473%	10.1%	205%	6.1%
High-income OECD countries	162%	3.5%	142%	3.0%

Notes: Scenario III. Simple averages of countries in each income group. See Tables 5.5 and C.1 for details.

The neoclassical estimates are taken as the lower bound on the effect of knowledge capital on future economic gains. Table 5.7 shows that the neoclassical model estimates for lower- and upper-middle income countries are roughly one-third lower in terms of percentage of discounted future GDP than the endogenous model estimates. That said, lower-middle income countries, as a group, can expect at least an 18% higher average GDP over the next 80 years, amounting to almost seven times the current GDP in these eight countries. The estimates for the neoclassical growth projections show a 10.7% higher average discounted GDP for the upper-middle income countries. For the high-income OECD countries, the gains are 3.0% instead of 3.5% of discounted future GDP.

The data do not permit distinguishing empirically between the two competing models of growth, but both alternatives suggest dramatic economic gains to be made for nations that meet the standard of universal basic skills.

MEASURES OF ECONOMIC INSTITUTIONS

Increasingly, discussions of economic growth and development have acknowledged the fundamental role of economic institutions in promoting or retarding development. For the past decade, a debate has also focused on the relative roles played by social institutions and by human capital.[19] This section explores whether consideration of various economic institutions affects the pattern of growth across nations as described above.

The analysis described here is not designed to resolve the divergent views about the predominance of institutions or about how precisely to measure the key economic institutions. Social institutions are almost certainly a component of differences in economic growth, and it is important to understand how they interact with countries' knowledge capital. But without seeking to resolve the debates, the analysis raises concerns about the measurement of human capital. Prior efforts to investigate the interaction between institutions and human capital across countries have carried out the analysis in terms of school attainment, something that is demonstrated to be an incomplete measure of the relevant skills of nations.

There are reasons to believe that the effect of cognitive skills may differ depending on the economic institutions of a country. The institutional framework plays an important role in shaping the relative profitability of piracy versus productive activity (North, 1990). If the available knowledge and skills are used in the former rather than the latter, the effect on economic growth is likely to be substantially different, and might even turn negative. Similarly, the allocation of talent between rent-seeking and entrepreneurship matters for economic growth: countries with relatively more engineering college majors have been shown to grow faster, and countries with relatively more law students to grow more slowly. (Murphy, Shleifer and Vishny, 1991).

Institutional barriers may also prevent skills from being properly allocated to different tasks on the labour market.(OECD, 2013a). Some have also argued that education may not have much impact in low-income countries that lack functioning markets and legal systems. In such countries, cognitive skills may be applied to socially unproductive activities, rendering the average effect of education on growth negligible (Easterly, 2001; Pritchett, 2001, 2006).

The authors have addressed elsewhere the estimation of how growth is affected by institutions; the results and implications are just summarised here. (Hanushek and Woessmann, 2015, section 3.2). Specifically, alternative measures of economic institutions are considered within the context of the basic growth models (see above). The approach is simply to add to the baseline models two common – and powerful – institutional measures related to the quality of the underlying economic environment: openness of the economy and security of property rights.[20] These measures are jointly significant in explaining growth, and the property rights measure is individually significant.[21] At the same time, the results show that cognitive skills continue to exert a positive and highly significant effect on economic growth independent of the measures related to the quality of institutions, although the estimated impact of cognitive skills is reduced from 2.0 to around 1.3, on average.

The estimation further adds an interaction term between cognitive skills and the two institutional measures. The results suggest that openness and cognitive skills not only have significant individual effects on economic growth but also show a significant positive interaction. This result is depicted in Figure 5.5.

FIGURE 5.5 HOW THE IMPACT OF KNOWLEDGE CAPITAL ON GROWTH VARIES BY ECONOMIC INSTITUTIONS

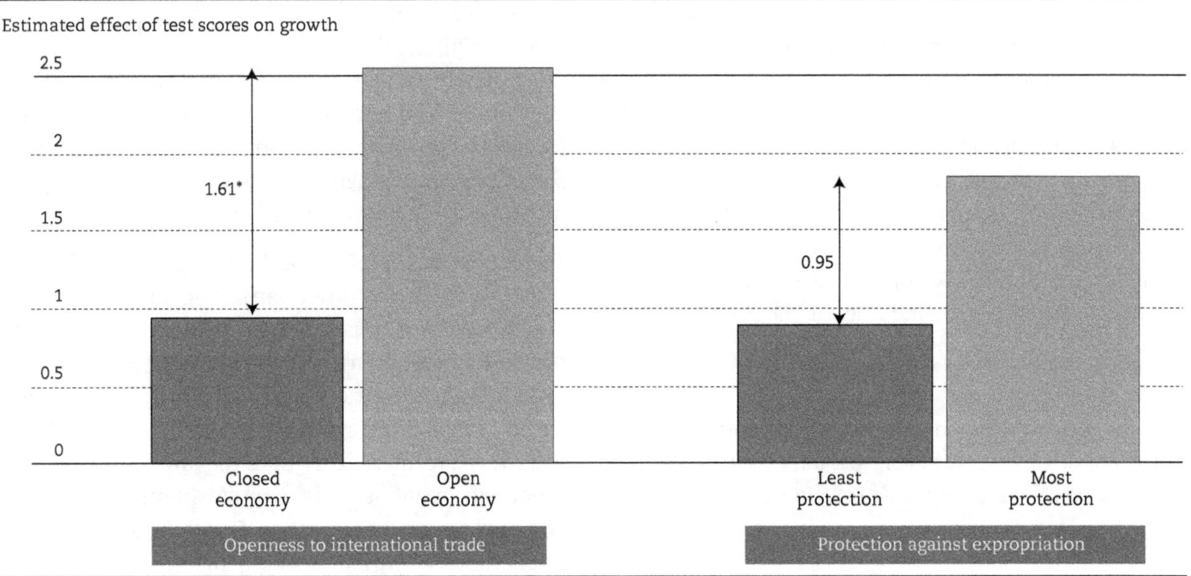

Notes: Estimated effect of average achievement test scores on the average annual rate of growth of real per capita GDP from 1960 to 2000, depending on the degree of openness to international trade and on the protection against expropriation risk of a country.

* Statistical significance at 5%.

Source: Hanushek and Woessmann (2015).

The effect of cognitive skills on economic growth is indeed significantly higher in countries that have been fully open to international trade than in countries that have been fully closed, though it is significantly positive in both. In closed economies, skills have a relatively low impact of 0.9 on growth rates, but the impact increases to 2.6 in open economies. When using protection against expropriation, rather than openness to trade, as the measure of quality of institutions, there is also a positive interaction term with cognitive skills, although it lacks statistical significance (Figure 5.5). Cognitive skills remain a significant determinant of growth differences. While the growth effects of knowledge capital are estimated to be reduced in the presence of institutional factors, the institutional measures include any effects of cognitive skills on the development of good institutions.

The overall interpretation in the context must be nuanced, since the high-income nations almost uniformly show no variation in either property rights or openness to international trade.[22] This suggests that developing countries with restrictive institutions have room for improving their economic performance by moving toward better institutions. But once they have, in fact, corrected the imperfect economic institutions, they too must return to relying on knowledge capital for any further improvements in growth.

Summary of the economic impacts of educational improvement

After considering the details of the separate policy movements, it is useful to put them all into perspective. In particular, it is instructive to compare Scenarios I-III, the three policy regimes: where all current students acquire basic skills; where universal enrolment is achieved at current quality levels; and where the goal of universal basic skills is achieved.

Table 5.8 summarises the results for the country groupings. Presenting the results by country grouping highlights how the impact and the policy implications vary across the groupings. For each grouping, the results in the table are in blocks based on the policy that is pursued.

TABLE 5.8 SUMMARY OF GAINS FROM SEPARATE POLICY OPTIONS

	Lower-middle income countries	Upper-middle income countries	High-income non-OECD countries	High-income OECD countries
Scenario I: All current students to basic skills				
In % of current GDP	627%	480%	362%	142%
In % of discounted future GDP	13.4%	10.3%	7.7%	3.0%
Long-run growth increase	0.83	0.66	0.50	0.21
Scenario II: Full enrolment at current quality				
In % of current GDP	206%	134%	60%	19%
In % of discounted future GDP	4.4%	2.9%	1.3%	0.4%
Long-run growth increase	0.30	0.20	0.09	0.03
Scenario III: Universal basic skills				
In % of current GDP	1302%	731%	473%	162%
In % of discounted future GDP	27.9%	15.6%	10.1%	3.5%
Long-run growth increase	1.42	0.94	0.63	0.24
Descriptive data				
Number of countries	8	23	14	31
Enrolment rate	0.752	0.830	0.930	0.977
Average score	395.4	410.7	460.8	502.0
Share below 420 points	0.585	0.545	0.355	0.201

Notes: Simple averages of countries in each income group. See Tables 5.3-5.5 for details.

Lower-middle income countries: Across the eight lower-middle income countries, if all current students attained the basic skills level, the present value of income gains would be over six times the current aggregate GDP of these countries. In these countries, 59% of students perform under the basic level of skills, consistent with an average achievement score of 395 PISA points. But historically the attention has been much more focused on ensuring universal access to school. While only 75% of youth are enrolled in secondary school in these countries, the gains from achieving universal access at current school quality are much smaller than those from raising achievement among current students: 4.4% of discounted future GDP for the former, compared to 13.4% for the latter. However, the third panel shows the extraordinary gains from ensuring universal basic skills – an increase of 27.9% in GDP (on average over the projection period) compared to what would be expected with current skill levels.[23]

Upper-middle income countries: The 23 upper-middle income countries in the sample are doing somewhat better than the lower-middle income countries in terms of enrolment rates (83%), achievement levels (411 points), and share of students who score below 420 points (54%). But the differences are not huge, and the economic impacts follow a pattern similar to that described for the lower-middle income group. The smallest impacts come from expanding enrolment at current school quality, larger impacts accrue from raising achievement levels among current students, and the largest, by far, come from achieving universal basic skills. Meeting this last goal yields an average growth dividend of seven times current GDP and would increase discounted future GDP by 15.6%, on average, over the economic outcomes of staying at the current education levels.

High-income non-OECD countries: The 14 high-income non-OECD countries represent a somewhat more heterogeneous grouping. The low enrolment rates in the Arab states of Bahrain (89%), Oman (82%) and Saudi Arabia (72%) imply the possibility of gains from expanded enrolment. But for these countries and for the group as a whole, the same pattern holds as for the two middle-income groupings: gains when current students acquire basic skills are greater than those when access to school is expanded, and the gains from achieving universal basic skills are greatest. Even for the oil states, then, more highly skilled populations have a significant impact on future growth and economic rewards.

High-income OECD countries: The high-income OECD countries are often left out of discussions of development goals. But these countries – with near universal secondary school enrolments – can make significant gains by improving education outcomes among the 20% of their students who score below Level 2. Enrolment expansion has little impact, but these 31 countries could see gains of 1.6 times current GDP, on average, and a 3.5% increase in discounted future GDP if all students acquired basic skills.

Of course, these projections have uncertainty imbedded in them. Alternative models and alternative interpretations of the underlying factors of growth can yield different estimates of the future. But in all cases, the economic gains from universal basic skills are large. These gains also very much overshadow the gains from just expanding access to schools at their current quality levels.

NOTES

1. The details of the projection methodology, in somewhat different circumstances, can be found in Hanushek and Woessmann (2011, 2015) and OECD, Hanushek and Woessmann (2010), where the authors focused on different policy scenarios (that do not take non-universal enrolment into account) just for OECD countries. Hanushek and Woessmann (2012) provided projections for European Union countries. Apart from the substantial expansion of country coverage, the clear focus of policy scenarios on reaching universal basic skills, and the treatment of less-than-universal participation, the main differences from the previous projection models are that reforms start in 2015 rather than 2010, that they take 15 rather than 20 years to complete, and that the growth coefficient is taken from a global, rather than OECD, sample.

2. The growth of the economy with the current level of skills is projected to be 1.5%, or the rough average of OECD growth over the past two decades.

3. The initial GDP refers to 2015 estimates based on PPP calculations in current international dollars; see International Monetary Fund (2014) [http://www.imf.org/external/pubs/ft/weo/2014/02/weodata/index.aspx (accessed 1/24/2015)].

4. For detailed descriptions of how Brazil, Korea and Turkey have achieved substantial improvements at different levels in PISA, see the respective boxes in this report and in OECD, 2013b.

5. The calculations take the weighted average of the 25-point gain for the proportion of young people enrolled in school and the zero gain for those who are not in school.

6. Hanushek and Woessmann (2015) analyse, across OECD countries, the long-run impact of a variety of labour and product market restrictions that are known to distort short-run economic decisions and outcomes. They find no discernible impact on long-run growth from these, but a pervasive impact of skill differences, suggesting that economies adjust to absorb increased skills of their workforces.

7. The 31 countries where girls outperform boys are Albania, Armenia, Bahrain, Botswana, Bulgaria, Cyprus (see note at the end of this chapter), Finland, Georgia, Greece, Iceland, Jordan, Kazakhstan, Latvia, Lithuania, Macedonia, Malaysia, Montenegro, Morocco, Norway, Oman, Qatar, Romania, the Russian Federation, Saudi Arabia, Singapore, Slovenia, South Africa, Sweden, Thailand, Turkey and the United Arab Emirates. See Table B.1 for details.

8. Assessing the impact of raising the performance for those who score below 420 points requires using the micro student data for each country. All analyses were performed separately for each of the five plausible values of the test scores and then averaged across the five plausible values.

9. In earlier work that estimated the impact on economic outcomes of various changes in knowledge capital, only OECD countries were considered where enrolment is not a serious issue and did not incorporate any school expansion. This omission was more serious for Mexico and Turkey, but the quality issues are themselves overwhelming. See Hanushek and Woessmann (2010, 2011, 2015).

10. Filmer, Hasan, and Pritchett (2006) pursue a different strategy of estimating performance from the distribution of PISA scores across grades (for the sampled 15-year-olds). There is currently no way to assess the validity of either this approach or that used in the projections here.

11. Knowledge capital thus increases by the difference between the current mean achievement and the current 25th percentile times the proportion of new enrollees.

12. These countries, in order of gain, are Ghana, Botswana, South Africa, Albania, Viet Nam, Macedonia, Iran, Lebanon and Colombia.

13. See the review and discussion in Hanushek and Woessmann (2015), section 8.4.

14. In order, OECD countries with gains exceeding twice GDP are Chile, Israel, the Slovak Republic, Greece, Italy, France, Sweden and Luxemburg.

15. The lowest secondary enrolment rates among high-income OECD countries are found in Chile (92%), Italy (94%), Greece (95%) and France (95%).

16. For additional sensitivity analyses of the projection models with respect to alternative parameter choices, see Hanushek and Woessmann (2011).

17. The standard description of the augmented neoclassical model can be found in Mankiw, Romer and Weil (1992). For a comparison of the alternatives, see Hanushek and Woessmann (2015).

18. The growth model is estimated with the logarithmic (rather than linear) initial per capita GDP as control. The test-score coefficient shows an imperceptible change in this specification (1.985 rather than 1.980), and the coefficient on log initial income is -0.879. With convergence, projections of growth rates with and without education reform will differ only during the transition to the new balanced growth path. The estimated convergence implies that a country will get halfway to a new steady state after 79 years. This is almost exactly the projection period employed here except that the projections show knowledge capital improvements that stretch out for 55 years.

19. In one influential line of research, Acemoglu, Johnson and Robinson (2001, 2005) have argued that major social institutions created the fundamental building blocks for modern development (see also Acemoglu, Gallego and Robinson [2014]). They particularly emphasise the centrality of strong property rights, arguing that the causal role of this institution can be seen analytically by tracing back the different colonial paths of different countries. On the other hand, Glaeser et al. (2004) have argued that the colonists brought human capital in addition to knowledge of good social institutions, and that it is more likely that better human capital led both to the development of good institutions and higher economic growth.

20. The measure of openness is the Sachs and Warner (1995) index. It reflects the fraction of years between 1960 and 1998 that a country was classified as having an economy open to international trade, based on five factors (tariffs, quotas, exchange rate controls, export controls, and whether or not a socialist economy). Following Acemoglu, Johnson and Robinson (2001), the measure of security of property rights is an index of the protection against expropriation risk, averaged over the period 1985-95, from Political Risk Services, a private company that assesses the risk that investments will be expropriated in different countries. Note that data limitations reduce the sample from 50 countries to 47.

21. Note that protection against expropriation and openness are strongly correlated, with a simple correlation of 0.71.

22. Having openness to trade and secure property rights does not, of course, imply that high-income countries uniformly employ the skills of their workers to the greatest extent possible. As a simple observation about the differences in use of skills, analysis of the PIAAC data of labour market earnings shows large differences in the productivity gains associated with greater skill. See the discussion in Chapter 6 and in Hanushek et al. (2015).

23. The gains in Scenario III are more than the simple addition of gains in Scenarios I and II because students who newly enter school do so in schools of higher quality than currently exist.

Notes regarding Cyprus

Readers should note the following information provided by Turkey and by the European Union Member States of the OECD and the European Union regarding the status of Cyprus:

Note by Turkey

The information in this document with reference to "Cyprus" relates to the southern part of the Island. There is no single authority representing both Turkish and Greek Cypriot people on the Island. Turkey recognises the Turkish Republic of Northern Cyprus (TRNC). Until a lasting and equitable solution is found within the context of the United Nations, Turkey shall preserve its position concerning the "Cyprus issue".

Note by all the European Union member States of the OECD and the European Union

The Republic of Cyprus is recognised by all members of the United Nations with the exception of Turkey. The information in this document relates to the area under the effective control of the Government of the Republic of Cyprus.

Note regarding Israel

The statistical data for Israel are supplied by and under the responsibility of the relevant Israeli authorities. The use of such data by the OECD is without prejudice to the status of the Golan Heights, East Jerusalem and Israeli settlements in the West Bank under the terms of international law.

REFERENCES

Acemoglu, D., F.A. Gallego and J.A. Robinson (2014), "Institutions, human capital, and development", *Annual Review of Economics*, Vol. 6, pp. 875-912.

Acemoglu, D., S. Johnson and J.A. Robinson (2005), "Institutions as a fundamental cause of long-run growth", in P. Aghion and S.N. Durlauf (eds.), *Handbook of Economic Growth*, Elsevier, Amsterdam, pp. 385-472.

Acemoglu, D., S. Johnson and J.A. Robinson (2001), "The colonial origins of comparative development: An empirical investigation", *American Economic Review*, Vol. 91/5, pp. 1369-1401.

Easterly, W. (2001), *The Elusive Quest for Growth: An Economist's Adventures and Misadventures in the Tropics*, The MIT Press, Cambridge, MA.

Filmer, D., A. Hasan and L. Pritchett (2006), "A millennium learning goal: Measuring real progress in education", *Working Paper*, No. 97, August, Center for Global Development, Washington, DC.

Glaeser, EL., R. La Porta, F. Lopez-de-Silanes and A. Shleifer (2004), "Do institutions cause growth?" *Journal of Economic Growth*, Vol. 9/3, pp. 271-303.

Hanushek, E.A. and L. Woessmann (2015), *The Knowledge Capital of Nations: Education and the Economics of Growth*, The MIT Press, Cambridge, MA.

Hanushek, E.A. and L. Woessmann (2012), "The economic benefit of educational reform in the European Union", *CESifo Economic Studies*, Vol. 58/1, pp. 73-109.

Hanushek, E.A. and L. Woessmann (2011), "How much do educational outcomes matter in OECD countries?" *Economic Policy*, Vol. 26/67, pp. 427-491.

IMF (2014), *World Economic Outlook*, International Monetary Fund, Washington, DC.

Mankiw, N.G., D. Romer and D. Weil (1992), "A contribution to the empirics of economic growth", *Quarterly Journal of Economics*, Vol. 107/2, pp. 407-437.

Murphy, K.M., A. Shleifer and R.W. Vishny (1991), "The allocation of talent: Implications for growth", *Quarterly Journal of Economics*, Vol. 106/2, pp. 503-530.

North, D.C. (1990), *Institutions, Institutional Change and Economic Performance*, Cambridge University Press, Cambridge.

OECD (2013a), *OECD Skills Outlook 2013: First Results from the Survey of Adult Skills*, OECD Publishing, Paris, http://dx.doi.org/10.1787/9789264204256-en.

OECD (2013b), *PISA 2012 Results: What Students Know and Can Do (Volume I, Revised edition, February 2014): Student Performance in Mathematics, Reading and Science*, OECD Publishing, Paris, http://dx.doi.org/10.1787/9789264208780-en.

OECD, E.A. Hanushek and L. Woessmann (2010), *The High Cost of Low Educational Performance: The Long-run Economic Impact of Improving PISA Outcomes*, PISA, OECD Publishing, Paris, http://dx.doi.org/10.1787/9789264077485-en.

Pritchett, L. (2006), "Does learning to add up add up? The returns to schooling in aggregate data", in E.A. Hanushek and F. Welch (eds.), *Handbook of the Economics of Education*, North Holland, Amsterdam, pp. 635-695.

Pritchett, L. (2001), "Where has all the education gone?" *World Bank Economic Review*, Vol. 15/3, pp. 367-391.

Sachs, J.D. and A.M. Warner (1995), "Economic reform and the process of global integration", *Brookings Papers on Economic Activity*, No. 1, pp. 1-96.

UNESCO (2014), *Teaching and Learning: Achieving Quality for All – EFA Global Monitoring Report 2013/4*. United Nations Educational, Scientific and Cultural Organization, Paris.

Chapter 6

Sharing the benefits of universal basic skills

This chapter discusses how the benefits of universal basic skills can be distributed across societies and can narrow gaps in earnings that feed into income disparities. It also considers the question of whether to support the lowest achievers and/or cultivate the highest achievers.

Inclusive growth has two components. Most broadly, it requires that all the countries of the world be in a position to reap the economic rewards from growth. This issue has been the focus of this report. But it also requires that the benefits of growth are shared among all citizens of each country. This latter distributional issue is also directly addressed by the development goal of universal basic skills because, as framed, the goal involves preparing all youth for participation in the global economy. Key distributional issues raised by this component – about how changing the skills distribution affects the income distribution, and about whether to focus on the basic-skills or the high-skills part of the skill distribution – are discussed below.

Variations in skills and in income

In any country, the observed income distribution is a function of many factors. The character of the labour market, the taxes levied by the government, the nature of any welfare and social security programmes, and the returns to investments all enter into the distribution of income. But in a modern competitive economy, a fundamental factor in determining incomes is the productivity of individuals that is rewarded in the labour market. Analysing the full distribution of income in the various economies of the world is clearly beyond the scope and intent of this report; but a look at how the distribution of productivity and individual earnings might change with achievement of universal basic skills is relevant, and can be undertaken using available data on skills distribution.

Simply put, the distribution of skills is an important ingredient in the distribution of productivity in modern economies, and in competitive economies the distribution of productivity directly affects the earnings of workers. The distribution of labour earnings, in turn, enters significantly into the distribution of income in society. Clearly the earnings distribution would change if all members of society had basic skills; but estimating this change is not possible for countries where the skills of significant shares of the population are not measured because their productivity and earnings are not known. Therefore, the estimation here is restricted to countries with a secondary school enrolment rate of 98% or more. For these countries, changes in the skills distribution brought about by universal basic skills are considered.

The most direct way to see these changes comes from information about the rewards to skills in the labour market. Information on labour market earnings is directly available for a number of OECD economies. Under the Survey of Adult Skills, a product of the OECD Programme for the International Assessment of Adult Competencies (PIAAC), the OECD sampled a random selection of adults in 24 countries in 2011-12 and gave them a series of tests covering cognitive skills in three domains: literacy, numeracy and problem solving in technology-rich environments. The tasks to be solved were often framed as real-world problems, such as maintaining a driver's logbook (numeracy domain) or reserving a meeting room on a particular date using a reservation system (problem-solving domain). The domains, described more completely in *OECD Skills Outlook 2013: First Results from the Survey of Adult Skills*, refer to key information-processing competencies that are demanded in modern economies.

Using the Survey of Adult Skills, it is possible to estimate how different skills affect individual earnings in different countries. It turns out that the return to skills varies considerably across countries.[1] The largest return to skills is found in the United States, and the analysis relies on estimates of the U.S. returns to indicate the impact of the improvements in skills discussed. This choice reflects the fact that the United States – with what is regarded generally as the least-distorted product and labour markets – is useful in identifying most clearly how individual skills affect productivity and potential earnings in the labour market.

The U.S. labour market data indicate that one standard deviation of mathematics achievement yields 28% higher earnings each year of a career, on average.[2] In other words, somebody at the 84th percentile of the mathematics distribution would earn 28% more than an average person (i.e. somebody at the 50th percentile) over their working lives. Similarly – and importantly for this analysis – somebody at the 16th percentile of the mathematics distribution would earn 28% less than an average person.

To see the changes that arise from attaining universal basic skills in terms of earnings, one can estimate the achievement-induced changes in the earnings distribution. The increase in average earnings from attaining a baseline level of skills amounts to some 4.2% across the 28 countries with universal enrolment in secondary schools.[3] This increase is accompanied by a 5.2% average reduction in the achievement-induced part of the standard deviation of earnings.[4] There is, however, considerable variation across countries: change is smallest in Estonia and Korea, and largest in Qatar and Tunisia.

This analysis points to a significant fact for inclusive development: achieving the development goal of universal basic skills has a complementary impact on reducing gaps in earnings that filter into income differences. But it has this impact while also expanding the size of the economy, and thus differs from simple tax and redistribution schemes that might change income distribution but would not add to societal output. Thus, policies to improve knowledge capital will also promote inclusion and a more equitable income distribution.

Basic skills for all and/or cultivating top achievers

One aspect of the previous calculations is artificial. It considers policies that affect only those youth who would otherwise not attain basic skills. The policies are analysed as if all others were unaffected, and this surely is an improbable outcome. Any school policy that improves the performance of the lowest achievers will likely improve the performance of some higher achievers as well. In this regard, then, the policy scenarios would represent lower bounds on the achievement and economic impacts of policies designed to ensure that all youth acquire at least basic skills (that is, at least 420 points on the Programme for International Student Assessment [PISA] proficiency scale).

A second aspect of the wider performance distribution also deserves attention. Many countries are torn between providing basic skills and cultivating the very highest achievers. Looking at the distribution of achievement within countries suggests that different countries make different choices about where to focus the attention of their education systems.[5]

Earlier research (Hanushek and Woessmann, 2015) compares economic growth under two scenarios: greater proportions of superior achievers and universal basic skills. Instead of relying on just mean skills, that analysis incorporates the share of top achievers (those who score above 600 points) and the share of bottom achievers (those who score less than 400 points) into the growth modeling. It turns out that at both ends of the distribution, a nation's cognitive skills are significantly related to economic growth, and this is true whether the two extremes are treated individually or jointly.[6] Both the basic-skill and the top-performing dimensions of education performance appear important for growth.

The impact of the basic-skills share does not vary significantly with the initial level of development, but the impact of the top-performing share is significantly larger in countries that have more scope to catch up to the most productive countries.[7] This difference appears to reflect the importance of high-skilled human capital in imitation strategies: the process of economic convergence is accelerated in countries with larger shares of high-performing students. Obvious cases are East Asian countries, such as Chinese Taipei, Singapore and Korea, all of which have particularly large shares of high performers, started from relatively low levels, and have shown outstanding growth. The interaction of the top-performing and basic-literacy shares in growth models appears to produce a complementarity between basic skills and top-level skills. In order to be able to implement the imitation and innovation strategies developed by the most-skilled workers, countries need a workforce with at least basic skills.

Many countries have focused on either promoting basic skills or producing engineers, scientists and other highly skilled workers. In terms of growth, the estimates described above suggest that these two efforts reinforce each other. Moreover, achieving basic literacy for all may well be a precondition for identifying those who can achieve at the highest levels. In other words, tournaments among a large pool of students with basic skills may be an efficient way to produce a large share of high performers.

Improving in PISA: Turkey

When it first participated in PISA, in 2003, Turkey was among the lowest-performing OECD countries in mathematics, reading and science. Yet Turkey's performance in all three domains has improved markedly since then, at an average yearly rate of 3.2, 4.1 and 6.4 points per year, respectively. In 2003, for example, the average 15-year-old student in Turkey scored 423 points in mathematics. With an average annual increase of 3.2 points, the average score in mathematics in 2012 was 448 points – an improvement over 2003 scores that is the equivalent of more than half a year of schooling. Much of this improvement was concentrated among students with the greatest educational needs. The mathematics scores of Turkey's lowest-achieving students (the 10th percentile) improved from 300 to 338 points between 2003 and 2012, with no significant change among the highest-achieving students during the period. Consistent with this trend, the share of students who perform below proficiency Level 2 in mathematics shrank from 52% in 2003 to 42% in 2012. Between-school differences in average mathematics performance did not change between 2003 and 2012, but differences in performance among students within schools narrowed during that time, meaning that much of the improvement in mathematics performance observed between 2003 and 2012 is the result of low-performing students across all schools improving their performance (Table II.2.1b).

The observed improvement in mathematics was concentrated among socio-economically disadvantaged and low-achieving students. Between 2003 and 2012, both the average difference in performance between advantaged and disadvantaged students and the degree to which students' socio-economic status predicts their performance shrank. In 2003, advantaged students outperformed disadvantaged students by almost 100 score points; in 2012, the difference was around 60 score points. In 2003, 28% of the variation in students' scores (around the OECD average) was explained by students' socio-economic status; by 2012, 15% of the variation (below the OECD average) was explained by students' socio-economic status. While all students, on average, improved their scores no matter where their schools were located, students attending schools in towns (population of 3 000 to 100 000) improved their mathematics scores by 59 points between 2003 and 2012 – more than the increase observed among students in cities or large cities (population greater than 100 000; no change in performance detected).

Turkey has a highly centralised school system: education policy is set centrally at the Ministry of National Education and schools have comparatively little autonomy. Education policy is guided by a two-year Strategic Plan and a four-year Development Plan. The Basic Education Programme (BEP), launched in 1998, sought to expand primary education, improve the quality of education and overall student outcomes, narrow the gender gap in performance, align performance indicators with those of the European Union, develop school libraries, ensure that qualified teachers were employed, integrate information and communication technologies into the education system, and create local learning centres, based in schools, that are open to everyone (OECD, 2007). The Master Implementation Plan (2001-05), designed in collaboration with UNICEF, and the Secondary Project (2006-11), in collaboration with the World Bank, included multiple projects to improve both equity and quality in the education system. The Standards for Primary Education, piloted in 2010 and recently expanded to all primary institutions, defines quality standards for primary education, guides schools in achieving these standards, develops a system of school self assessments, and guides local and central authorities in addressing inequalities among schools.

Compulsory education law

One of the major changes introduced with the BEP programme involved the compulsory education law. This change was first implemented in the 1997/98 school year, and in 2003 the first students graduated from the eight-year compulsory education system. Since the launch of this programme, the attendance rate among primary students increased from around 85% to nearly 100%, while the attendance rate in pre-primary programmes increased from 10% to 25%. In addition, the system was expanded to include 3.5 million more pupils, average class size was reduced to roughly 30 students, all students learn at least one foreign language, computer laboratories were established in every primary school, and overall physical conditions were improved in all 35 000 rural schools. Resources devoted to the programme exceeded USD 11 billion. This programme did not directly affect school participation for most of the 15-year-olds assessed by PISA, who are mainly in secondary schools where enrolment rates are close to 60%. In 2012, compulsory education was increased from 8 to 12 years of schooling, and the school system was redefined into three levels (primary, lower secondary and upper secondary) of four years each.

Fifteen-year-old students in Turkey are the least likely among students in all OECD countries to have attended pre-primary education. Several initiatives are in place to change this, but none has yet had a direct impact on the students who participated in PISA 2012. Early childhood education and care is featured in the current Development Plan (2014-18) and other on-going programmes include the Mobile Classroom (for children aged 36-66 months from low-income families), the Summer Preschool (for children aged 60-66 months), the Turkey Country Programme, and the Pre-School Education Project.

Improving in PISA: Turkey (continued)

Curricular reform

New curricula were introduced in the 2006/07 school year, starting from the 6th grade. The secondary school mathematics and language curricula were also revised and a new science curriculum was applied in the 9th grade for the 2008/09 school year. In PISA 2012 students had already been taught the new curriculum for four years, although their primary school education was part of the former system. The standards of the new curricula were intended to meet PISA goals: "Increased importance has been placed on students' doing mathematics which means exploring mathematical ideas, solving problems, making connections among mathematical ideas, and applying them in real life situations" (Talim ve Terbiye Kurulu [TTKB] [Board of Education], 2008).

The curricular reform was designed not only to change the content of school education and encourage the introduction of innovative teaching methods, but above all to change the teaching philosophy and culture within schools. The new curricula and teaching materials emphasise "student-centred learning", giving students a more active role than before, when memorising information had been the predominant approach. They also reflect the assumption, on which PISA is based, that schools should equip students with the skills needed to ensure success at school and in life, in general.

In 2003, more than one in four students reported having arrived late for school at least once in the two weeks prior to the PISA test; by 2012, more than four in ten students reported having arrived late. By contrast, students' sense of belonging at school seems to have improved during the same period. Students in 2012 also spent half an hour less per week in mathematics instruction than students in 2003 did, and almost an hour-and-a-half less per week in after-school study.

Changes in the schools

Students in 2012 attended schools with better physical infrastructure and better educational resources than their counterparts in 2003 did. Throughout 2004 and 2005, private-sector investments funded 14 000 additional classrooms in the country. Taxes were reduced for private businesses that invested in education. This was particularly helpful in provinces where there was large internal migration (OECD, 2006).

Several policies had sought to change the culture and management of schools. Schools were obliged to propose a plan of work, including development targets and strategic plans for reaching them. More democratic governance, parental involvement and teamwork were suggested. In 2004, a project aimed at teaching students democratic skills was started in all primary and secondary schools, with many responsibilities assigned to student assemblies. In addition, more transparent and performance-oriented inspection tools were introduced.

Teachers were also the target of policy changes. New arrangements were implemented in 2008 to train teachers for upper secondary education through five-year graduate programmes. The arrangements also stipulated that graduates in other fields, such as science or literature, who wanted to teach would also have to attend a year-and-a-half of graduate training in education. The Teacher Formation Programmes of Education Faculties (2008) links pre-service training courses to the Ministry's curriculum and teacher-practice standards while giving more autonomy to faculties on the courses that should be taught. The New Teacher Programme, introduced in 2011, established stricter requirements for certain subjects.

Several projects implemented over the past decade have addressed equity issues. The Girls to Schools Now campaign, in collaboration with UNICEF, that started in 2003 aimed to ensure that all girls aged 6 to 14 attend primary school. Efforts to increase enrolment in school continue through programmes like the Address-Based Population Registry System, which creates a registry to identify non-schooled children, the Education with Transport programme, which benefits students who have no access to school, and the Complementary Transitional Training Programme, which tries to ensure that 10-14 year-olds acquire a basic education even if they have never been enrolled in a school or if they had dropped out of school. The Project for Increasing Enrolment Rates Especially for Girls, in a pilot phase in the 16 provinces with the lowest enrolment rates among girls, addresses families' awareness about the links between education and the labour market. Since 2003, textbooks for all primary students have been supplied free of charge by the Ministry of National Education. The International Inspiration Project, begun in 2011, and the Strengthening Special Education Project, begun in 2010, are designed to promote disadvantaged students' performance.

Sources:

OECD (2013), *Education Policy Outlook: Turkey*, OECD Publishing, Paris, *http://www.oecd.org/edu/EDUCATION%20POLICY%20OUTLOOK%20TURKEY_EN.pdf*

OECD (2007), *Reviews of National Policies for Education: Basic Education in Turkey*, OECD Publishing, Paris, *http://dx.doi.org/10.1787/9789264030206-en*

OECD (2006), *Economic Survey of Turkey: 2006*, OECD Publishing, Paris, *http://dx.doi.org/10.1787/eco_surveys-tur-2006-en*

Talim ve Terbiye Kurulu (TTKB) (2008), *sIkögretim Matematik Dersi 6–8 Sınıflar Öğretim Programı ve Kılavuzu (Teaching Syllabus and Curriculum Guidebook for Elementary School Mathematics Course: Grades 6 to 8)*, Milli Eğitim Bakanlığı, Ankara.

NOTES

1. See the analysis in Hanushek et al. (2015). This analysis also shows that earnings within each country are related to the individual's years of schooling. This differs from the international growth analysis, where school attainment has no impact on growth after consideration is given to cognitive skills. Hanushek and Woessmann (2012) explain this apparent anomaly by showing that human capital investments by individuals may signal skill differences when compared to other workers in an economy, but there is no relationship between the level of school quality and the steepness of the returns to school investments within a country.

2. The analysis of the PIAAC data indicates a wide range of returns to mathematics skills – from 28% in the United States to 12% in Sweden.

3. The list of countries, along with changes in the mean and standard deviation of achievement based on reaching basic skills, is found in Table D.1 in Annex D. The earnings gains come from relating the change in skills to earnings through the estimated U.S. earnings parameter of 28% per standard deviation.

4. In calculating the standard deviation of the post-reform distribution, a score of 420 points is assigned to everybody previously below this level. In reality, instead of all of the people being stacked at 420 points, there would almost certainly be a distribution of scores, with a portion of the affected distribution scoring above 420 points. This would produce an even larger reduction in the standard deviation than calculated here.

5. See the depictions of distributions of cognitive skills across countries in Hanushek and Woessmann (2015), section 3.3.

6. In the joint model, the two measures are separately significant even though they are highly correlated across countries, with a simple correlation of 0.73.

7. The larger growth effect of high-level skills in countries farther from the technological frontier is most consistent with technological diffusion models (e.g. Nelson and Phelps, 1966).

REFERENCES

Hanushek, E.A., G. Schwerdt, S. Wiederhold and L. Woessmann (2015), "Returns to skills around the world: Evidence from PIAAC", *European Economic Review*, Vol. 73, pp. 103-130.

Hanushek, E.A. and L. Woessmann (2015), *The Knowledge Capital of Nations: Education and the Economics of Growth*, The MIT Press, Cambridge, MA.

Nelson, R.R. and E. Phelps (1966), "Investment in humans, technology diffusion and economic growth", *American Economic Review*, Vol. 56/2, pp. 69-75.

OECD (2013), *OECD Skills Outlook 2013: First Results from the Survey of Adult Skills*, OECD Publishing, Paris, http://dx.doi.org/10.1787/9789264204256-en.

Chapter 7

What achieving universal basic skills means for the economy and for education

A fundamental education goal for all nations can be succinctly stated: all youth should acquire at least basic skills. This chapter summarises the benefits – both economic and social – that could accrue to countries, rich and poor, if their populations were to acquire basic skills.

There are two types of conclusions that can be drawn from this report. The first relates to what the analysis has to say about the economic benefits of the development goal of achieving universal basic skills. The second relates to the connection of this goal to larger education policies.

The Millennium Development Goals for education were successful in that they led to some significant expansion in access to education, particularly in the developing world. But they were less successful in realising a commensurate expansion in the achievement, or knowledge capital, of nations. It was for this reason that many of the hoped-for outcomes, particularly for economic development, failed to materialise.

It is relatively easy to mobilise support for development goals in education, both within individual countries and among international development agencies, because there is ready acceptance of the idea that nations' growth is directly related to human capital – the skills of the populations. The disappointments have come largely from an undue focus on access to schooling as opposed to learning while in school. Assessing progress towards education goals by measuring years of schooling attained gives an incomplete picture. Over the past two decades, school attainment has grown significantly, but learning has not grown commensurately.

This report builds on prior work that focuses on the gains from learning and that supports the finding of a strong, causal relationship between cognitive skills and economic growth.[1] A fundamental education goal for all nations can be succinctly stated: all youth should acquire at least basic skills. A workable definition of basic skills in today's economically competitive world is fully mastering skills at Level 1 on the Programme for International Student Assessment (PISA) test, which is equivalent to a mathematics score of 420 points. This quality aspect of the education goal can be readily measured and tracked, thus providing a similar impetus to development as did the prior focus on attainment.

The history of economic growth makes understanding the economic implications of different education policies straightforward. Three options that represent much of current policy discussion can be readily compared (see Chapter 5): all current students with basic skills; universal access to schools at current quality; and universal access with basic skills.

Universal access at current quality yields some economic gains, particularly in the lower-income countries. But improving the quality of schools to raise achievement for current students has a much larger economic impact. Meeting the goal of universal access with basic skills has an even greater impact. For lower-middle income countries, the discounted present value of future gains would be 13 times current GDP and would average out to a 28% higher GDP over the next 80 years. For upper-middle income countries, it would average out to a 16% higher GDP.

The goal of universal basic skills also has meaning for high-income countries. Driven in part by oil-producing countries that face some schooling challenges, the high-income non-OECD countries, as a group, would see an average of 10% higher future GDP – almost five times the value of current GDP – if they met this goal. And even the high-income OECD countries would gain significantly if all segments of the population acquired basic skills. For this group, average future GDP would be 3.5% higher than it would be otherwise. Improving the skills of the population clearly has substantial implications for economic well-being, in particular when improvements that accrue in the more distant future are also considered.

When these gains are compared to the total spending on education – typically 3-5% of GDP – arguments against school improvement based on limited funds are indeed shortsighted. The gains from meeting the goal of universal basic skills would cover most, if not all, of the costs of the entire education system, even in the most developed economies.[2]

Available evidence suggests that schools and student achievement can be improved, even though countries have found improvement difficult in the past. Figure 7.1 depicts the average improvement over the past 15 years (for nations that have participated sufficiently in testing to provide longitudinal data on performance).[3] The pace of the top performers yields dramatic changes in their knowledge capital. A four-point-per-year improvement over the 14 years of observation implies an improvement of greater than a half standard deviation – or twice the improvement that was analysed in the baseline projection. All of the countries in the graph from Italy up to Latvia have managed to gain at least 25 points. Of course, nine countries also fell back in achievement over the period shown.[4] Their experience illustrates that improvement can be difficult.

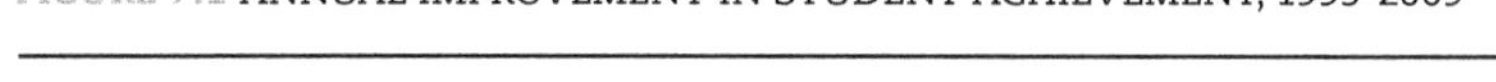

FIGURE 7.1 ANNUAL IMPROVEMENT IN STUDENT ACHIEVEMENT, 1995-2009

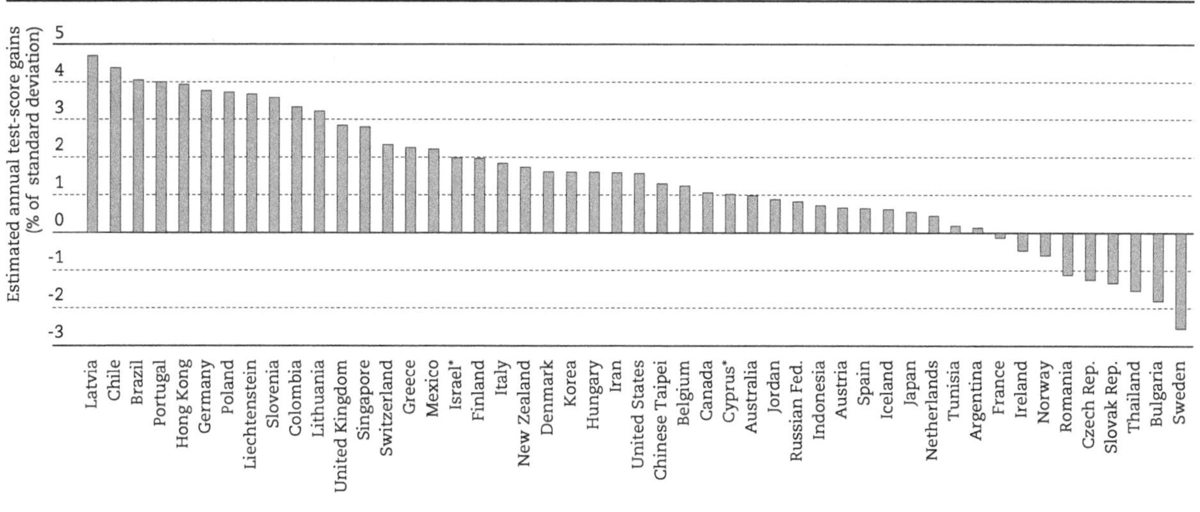

* See notes at the end of this chapter.

Notes: Estimated annual test-score change as % of a standard deviation, based on NAEP, PISA, TIMSS and PIRLS achievement tests.

Source: Hanushek, Peterson and Woessmann (2012), Table B.1.

Countries currently at the bottom of the overall skills distribution will not find it possible to reach the goal of universal basic skills within a 15-year period, no matter how aggressively they seek to improve their schools. Acknowledging that this is so, however, represents neither a retreat from the goal nor a reason to ignore it. As described in Chapter 5, stretching achievement of the goal to 30 years instead of 15 years leads to some obvious reduction in the gains – but the gains remain enormous, particularly compared to current levels of income. And such rewards cannot easily be obtained by any alternative policies.

This is not the place to develop the evidence on alternative improvement policies, but a few lessons that clearly relate to this analysis can be mentioned.[5] Perhaps the most important lesson is that improvement is not possible without a clear set of goals. Policies must be related to objectives. In fact, the report provides direct evidence of how goals do lead to outcomes; the rapid expansion of access to schools in the face of the original Millennium Development Goal – universal primary schooling – reinforces this proposition.

The past expansion of access also highlights the central theme of this report. Getting children into schools was not the real purpose of the goal; it was a means to the true end of increasing the learning and achievement of all youth. But because the goal was not framed in terms of learning outcomes, improvements in access did not necessarily lead to general learning gains. As this report has shown, increased educational attainment without increased learning has limited impact on economic outcomes and on development.

It is equally clear that meeting policy objectives and goals is unlikely without measuring performance. Without information about student achievement, it is impossible to judge accurately whether programmes are meeting their real objectives. The strength of the prior access goals was that performance could be readily measured. At this point, the goals that more directly reflect the true objectives can also be accurately measured.

Judging the overall performance of the school system in today's internationally linked economic markets requires accurate assessments of performance by international standards. There is now a half century of experience with international testing, and this provides participating nations with a view of how their current performance measures up against what is possible.[6] These international tests feed directly into the development goal of universal basic skills. Basic skills today can be defined only by international standards. Moreover, within countries, it is unlikely that people without basic skills can be included in the gains of any development.

The analysis in this report focuses on the 76 countries with comparable international achievement data, and there is reason to believe that many of the countries that do not participate in international assessments perform worse than even the lower-performing countries. Countries participating in regional testing in Latin America and in sub-Saharan Africa provide wider evidence of substandard outcomes for non-participating countries. If inclusive growth is to reach the poorest countries and regions, the measurement of outcomes for them must be widely expanded.

A frequent argument against pursuit of universal basic skills is that it is simply too costly. Yet, among the middle-income countries, the gains of reaching this goal average more than 6% of discounted future GDP everywhere except Hungary (where it is 4.1%).[7] These gains, the average over the next 80 years, exceed the total current expenditures on education in these countries, indicating considerable room for investment. Of course, there may still be short-run budgetary pressures, since it will be necessary first to improve schools and then to wait while high-skilled youth become a significant portion of the labour force. Nevertheless, forward-looking governments must understand that changing the economic future requires investment.

One caution to keep in mind is that the economic gains come only with the development of higher achievement and higher skills. Investment in education is often understood just in terms of spending; but higher spending is not necessarily the same as higher achievement, as the record across countries shows.[8] Numerous programmes and policies that sound good and that have been introduced by governments in good faith have turned out to be ineffective at raising achievement, leading to increased cost with little gain.

As the record shows, the economic development that follows from reaching universal basic skills would contribute to poverty reduction, better health care, development of new and sustainable technologies, and other improvements that come with increased resources. Or to put this the other way, only improved knowledge capital makes these larger social goals feasible.

NOTES

1. The underlying support for the basic growth model is found in Hanushek and Woessmann (2015). It is summarised in Chapter 2 and Annex A.

2. In 2010, public spending on primary and secondary schools within OECD countries averaged 3.7% of GDP; see OECD (2013).

3. For a discussion of how improvement is calculated, see Hanushek, Peterson and Woessmann (2012).

4. Those that regressed were Bulgaria, the Czech Republic, France, Ireland, Norway, Romania, the Slovak Republic, Sweden and Thailand.

5. See Chapter 8 in Hanushek and Woessmann (2015) and the references therein for international evidence on policy effectiveness.

6. The history of testing and participation by nations can be found in Hanushek and Woessmann (2011).

7. In the high-income OECD countries, the smallest gain in terms of future discounted GDP is found in Estonia (1.1%), but 18 of the 31 countries would see an improvement of over 3%.

8. See Hanushek and Woessmann (2015), section 8.1.

Notes regarding Cyprus

Readers should note the following information provided by Turkey and by the European Union Member States of the OECD and the European Union regarding the status of Cyprus:

Note by Turkey

The information in this document with reference to "Cyprus" relates to the southern part of the Island. There is no single authority representing both Turkish and Greek Cypriot people on the Island. Turkey recognises the Turkish Republic of Northern Cyprus (TRNC). Until a lasting and equitable solution is found within the context of the United Nations, Turkey shall preserve its position concerning the "Cyprus issue".

Note by all the European Union member States of the OECD and the European Union

The Republic of Cyprus is recognised by all members of the United Nations with the exception of Turkey. The information in this document relates to the area under the effective control of the Government of the Republic of Cyprus.

Note regarding Israel

The statistical data for Israel are supplied by and under the responsibility of the relevant Israeli authorities. The use of such data by the OECD is without prejudice to the status of the Golan Heights, East Jerusalem and Israeli settlements in the West Bank under the terms of international law.

REFERENCES

Hanushek, E. A. and L. Woessmann (2015), *The Knowledge Capital of Nations: Education and the Economics of Growth*, The MIT Press, Cambridge, MA.

Hanushek, E. A. and L. Woessmann (2011), "The economics of international differences in educational achievement", in *Handbook of the Economics of Education*, Vol. 3, edited by E. A. Hanushek, S. Machin and L. Woessmann, Amsterdam, pp. 89-200.

Hanushek, E. A., P. E. Peterson and L. Woessmann (2012), *Achievement Growth: International and U.S. State Trends in Student Achievement*, Program on Education Policy and Governance, Harvard Kennedy School, Cambridge, MA.

OECD (2013), *Education at a Glance 2013: OECD Indicators*, OECD Publishing, Paris, http://dx.doi.org/10.1787/eag-2013-en.

Annexes

Annex A REVIEW OF KNOWLEDGE CAPITAL AND GROWTH

Annex B TRANSFORMING PERFORMANCE IN TIMSS ONTO THE PISA SCALE

Annex C AUGMENTED NEOCLASSICAL RESULTS

Annex D DISTRIBUTION OF SKILLS WHEN GOAL OF UNIVERSAL BASIC SKILLS IS ACHIEVED

Annex E SAMPLE OF PISA QUESTIONS REQUIRING LEVEL 1 SKILLS

Annex A

Review of knowledge capital and growth

This annex provides a more technical overview of the estimates of growth models that are relied upon in the text. It also describes the various tests used to judge whether the estimates can be interpreted as causal estimates of the effect of knowledge capital. More detail is found in Hanushek and Woessmann (2015).

Basic growth model estimates

Prior theoretical and empirical work has pursued a variety of specifications of the underlying growth process.[1] Because the economic analysis of this report relies heavily on the estimates of growth models, it is useful to have an overview of these.

A country's growth rate can be considered as a function of workers' skills along with other systemic factors, including economic institutions and initial levels of income and technology. Skills are frequently referred to simply as the workers' human capital stock.

$$growth = \alpha_1 human\ capital + \alpha_2 other\ factors + \varepsilon \quad (1)$$

This formulation suggests that nations with more human capital tend to continue to make greater productivity gains than nations with less human capital, although the possibility is considered that the induced growth in productivity disappears over time.[2]

The empirical macroeconomic literature focusing on cross-country differences in economic growth has overwhelmingly employed measures related to school attainment, or years of schooling, to test the human capital aspects of growth models. It has tended to find a significant positive association between quantitative measures of schooling and economic growth.[3]

Nevertheless, these formulations introduce substantial bias into the picture of economic growth. Average years of schooling is a particularly incomplete and potentially misleading measure of education for comparing the impacts of human capital on the economies of different countries. It implicitly assumes that a year of schooling delivers the same increase in knowledge and skills regardless of the education system. For example, a year of schooling in Brazil is assumed to create the same increase in productive human capital as a year of schooling in Korea.[4] Formulations relying on this measure also assume that formal schooling is the only source of education, and that variations in non-school factors have negligible effects on education outcomes and skills. This neglect of cross-country differences in the quality of schools and in the strength of family, health and other influences is probably the major drawback of such a quantitative measure of schooling.

The role of other influences is in fact acknowledged in a standard version of an education production function as employed in extensive literature.[5] This formula expresses skills as a function of a range of factors:

$$human\ capital = \beta_1 schools + \beta_2 families + \beta_3 ability + \beta_4 health + \beta_5 other\ factors + \upsilon \quad (2)$$

In general, human capital combines both school attainment and school quality with the other relevant factors, including education in the family, health, labour market experience and so forth.

Thus, while school attainment has been a convenient measure to use in empirical work because the data are readily available across countries, its use ignores differences in school quality in addition to other important determinants of people's skills. A more satisfying alternative is to incorporate variations in cognitive skills, which can be determined through international assessments of mathematics, science and reading achievement, as a direct measure of the human capital input into empirical analyses of economic growth.

The focus on cognitive skills has a number of potential advantages. First, it captures variations in the knowledge and ability that schools strive to produce, and thus relates the putative outputs of schooling to subsequent economic success. Second, by emphasising total outcomes of education, it incorporates skills from any source – including families and innate ability as well as schools. Third, by allowing for differences in performance among students whose schooling differs in quality (but possibly not in quantity), it acknowledges – and invites investigation of – the effect of different policies on school quality. Fourth, it is practical in that data are readily available through consistent and reliable cross-country assessments.

The growth analysis relies on the measures of cognitive skills developed in Hanushek and Woessmann (2015). Between 1964 and 2003, 12 different international tests of math, science or reading were administered to a voluntarily participating group of countries.[6] These tests produce 36 different possible scores for subject-year-age combinations (e.g. science for students of grade 8 in 1972 as part of the First International Science Study, or mathematics for 15-year-olds in 2000 as a part of the first test in the Programme for International Student Assessment [PISA]). The assessments were designed to identify a common set of expected skills, which were then tested in the local language. Each test is newly constructed, until recently with no effort to link to any of the other tests. Hanushek and Woessmann (2015) describe the construction of consistent measures at the national level across countries through empirical calibration of the different tests.[7] These measures of knowledge capital for nations rely on the average (standardised) test scores for each country's historical participation in the tests. The aggregate scores are scaled (like PISA today) to have a mean of 500 and a standard deviation at the individual level of 100 across OECD countries.

The test scores can be interpreted as an index of the human capital of the population of each country. This interpretation of averages over different cohorts is reasonable if a country's scores have been stable across time – that is, if estimates from recent school-aged populations provide an estimate of the older working population.[8] If scores (and skills) change over time, some measurement error is clearly introduced. Scores have, in fact, changed somewhat, but within the period of observations, differences in levels across countries dominate any intertemporal score changes.[9]

Based on the more refined measure of human capital found in the aggregate test scores for each country, equation (1) can be estimated.[10] Table A.1 presents the basic results on the association between education outcomes and long-run economic growth in the sample of 50 countries for which both economic growth data and measures of knowledge capital are available.[11] The inclusion of initial per capita GDP in all specifications simply reflects the fact that it is easier for countries to grow when they are farther from the technology frontier, because they need only imitate others rather than invent new things.

TABLE A.1 BASIC GROWTH REGRESSIONS: LONG-RUN GROWTH IN PER CAPITA GDP, 1960-2000

	(1)	(2)	(3)
Cognitive skills		2.015***	1.980***
		(10.68)	(9.12)
Initial years of schooling (1960)	0.369***		0.026
	(3.23)		(0.34)
Initial per capita GDP (1960)	-0.379***	-0.287***	-0.302***
	(4.24)	(9.15)	(5.54)
Constant	2.785***	-4.827***	-4.737***
	(7.41)	(6.00)	(5.54)
Number of countries	50	50	50
R2 (adj.)	0.252	0.733	0.728

Notes: Dependent variable: average annual growth rate in per capita GDP, 1960 to 2000. Cognitive skill measure refers to average score on all international tests 1964 to 2003 in mathematics and science, primary through end of secondary school. t-Statistics in parentheses: statistical significance at *** 1%. Source: Hanushek and Woessmann (2015).

When knowledge capital is ignored (column 1 of Table A.1), years of schooling in 1960 is significantly associated with average annual growth rates in real per capita GDP in 1960-2000.[12] However, once the test measure of human capital is included (columns 2 and 3), cognitive skills are highly significant, and years of schooling become statistically insignificant, as the estimated coefficient drops to close to zero. Furthermore, the variation in cross-country growth explained by the model increases from 25% to 73% when human capital is measured by cognitive skills rather than years of schooling. Note that the bivariate association with initial per capita GDP already accounts for 7% of the variance in subsequent growth. All the more remarkable, then, is the relative increase in understanding growth that comes from including cognitive skills over what would be seen from just the natural convergence of growth as countries move toward greater development.

The estimated coefficient on cognitive skills implies that an increase of one standard deviation in educational achievement (i.e. 100 score points on the PISA scale) yields an average annual growth rate over the 40 years of observation that is two percentage points higher. This historical experience suggests a very powerful response to improvements in education outcomes, particularly when compared to the average 2.3% annual growth within the sampled countries over the past two decades.

Causality in brief

The fundamental question the analysis raises is this: should this tight relationship between cognitive skills and economic growth be interpreted as a causal one that can support direct policy actions?[13] In other words, if achievement were raised, would growth rates be expected to go up by a commensurate amount?

Work on differences in growth among countries, while extensive over the past two decades, has been plagued by legitimate questions about whether any truly causal effects have been identified, or whether the estimated statistical analyses simply pick up a correlation that emerges for other reasons.

Knowing that the relationship is causal, and not simply a byproduct of some other factors, is clearly important from a policy standpoint. Policymaking requires confidence that by improving academic achievement, countries will bring about a corresponding improvement in the long-run growth rate. If the relationship between test scores and growth rates simply reflects other factors that are correlated with both test scores and growth rates, policies designed to raise test scores may have little or no impact on the economy.

The early studies that found positive effects of years of schooling on economic growth may well have been suffering from reverse causality; they correctly identified a relationship between improved growth and more schooling, but incorrectly saw the latter as the cause and not the effect.[14] In this case, the data may have reflected the fact that as a country gets richer, it tends to buy more of many things, including more years of schooling for its population.

There is less reason to think that higher student achievement is caused by economic growth. For one thing, scholars have found little impact of additional education spending on achievement outcomes, so it is unlikely that the relationship comes from growth-induced resources lifting student achievement.[15] Still, it remains difficult to develop conclusive tests of causality with the limited sample of countries included in the analysis.

The best way to increase the confidence that higher student achievement results in economic growth is explicitly to consider alternative explanations of the observed achievement-growth relationship to determine whether plausible alternatives that could confound the results can be ruled out. No single approach can address all of the important concerns. But a combination of approaches – if together they provide support for a causal relationship between achievement and growth – can offer some assurance that the potentially problematic issues are not affecting the results.

POTENTIAL PROBLEMS IN IDENTIFYING CAUSALITY

The following summarises the authors' investigations into the potential problems with the prior estimation and their likely severity. These have been more fully reported elsewhere.[16]

First, other factors besides cognitive skills may be responsible for countries' economic growth. In an extensive investigation of alternative model specifications, different measures of cognitive skills, various groupings of countries (including some that eliminate regional differences), and specific sub-periods of economic growth have been employed. But the results show a consistency in the alternative estimates, in both quantitative impacts and statistical significance, that is uncommon in cross-country growth modeling. Nor do measures of geographical location, political stability, capital stock and population growth significantly affect the estimated impact of cognitive skills. These specification tests rule out some basic problems attributable to omitted causal factors that have been noted in prior growth work. Of course, there are other possible omitted factors, leading to a deeper investigation of the details of international differences.

Second, the most obvious reverse-causality issues arise because the analysis relates growth rates over the period 1960 to 2000 to test scores for roughly the same period. To address this directly, the period of the testing is separated from the period of observed economic impacts. Test scores through 1984 are related to economic growth in the period since 1985 (until 2009). In this analysis, available for a sample of 25 countries only, test scores strictly pre-date the growth period, making it clear that increased growth could not be causing the higher test scores. This estimation shows a positive effect of early test scores on subsequent growth rates that is almost twice as large as that displayed above. Indeed, this fact itself may be significant, because it is consistent with the possibility that skills have become even more important for the economy in recent periods.

Third, even if reverse causality is not an issue, one cannot be sure that the important international differences in test scores reflect school policies. After all, differences in achievement may arise because of health and nutrition differences in the population or simply because of cultural differences regarding learning and testing. This concern can be addressed by focusing attention just on the variations in achievement that arise directly from institutional characteristics of each country's school system (exit examinations, autonomy, relative teacher salaries and private schooling).[17] When the analysis is limited in this way, the estimation of the growth relationship yields essentially the same results as previously presented. The similarity of the results supports the causal interpretation of the effect of cognitive skills as well as the conclusion that schooling policies can have direct economic returns.

Fourth, a possible alternative to the conclusion that high achievement drives economic growth not eliminated by the prior analysis is that countries with good economies also have good school systems. In this case, achievement is simply a reflection of other important aspects of the economy and not the driving force in growth.

One simple way to test this possibility is to consider the implications of differences in measured skills within a single economy, thus eliminating institutional or cultural factors that may make the economies of different countries grow faster. This can readily be done by comparing immigrants to the United States who have been educated in their home countries with immigrants educated just in the United States. Since the two groups are within the single labour market of the United States, any differences in labour market returns associated with cognitive skills cannot arise from differences in the economy or culture of their home country.

This comparison finds that the cognitive skills seen in the immigrant's home country lead to higher incomes, but only if the immigrant was in fact educated in the home country. Immigrants from the same home country who are schooled in the United States see no economic return to home-country test scores – a finding that pinpoints the value of better schools. These results hold when Mexicans (the largest U.S. immigrant group) are excluded and when only immigrants from English-speaking countries are included. While not free from problems, this comparative analysis rules out the possibility that test scores simply reflect cultural factors or economic institutions of the home country.[18] It also lends further support to the potential role of schools in changing the cognitive skills of citizens in economically meaningful ways.

CHANGES OVER TIME

Perhaps the toughest test of causality is relating changes in test scores over time to changes in growth rates. If test-score improvements actually lead to an increase in growth rates, it should show up in such a relationship. For those countries that have participated in testing at different points over the past half century, one can observe whether students seem to be getting better or worse over time. (For more recent periods, the report examines changes over time in detail in Chapter 7). This approach implicitly eliminates country-specific economic and cultural factors because it looks at what happens over time within each country.

For 12 OECD countries, the magnitude of trends in education performance can be related to the magnitude of trends in growth rates over time.[19] This investigation provides more evidence of the causal influence of cognitive skills, although the small number of countries is obviously problematic. The gains in test scores over time are very closely related to the gains in growth rates over time.[20] Like the other approaches, this analysis must presume that the pattern of achievement changes has been occurring over a long time, because it is not the achievement of school children but the skills of workers that count. Nonetheless, the consistency of the patterns is striking.

Again, each approach to determining causation is subject to its own uncertainty. Nonetheless, the combined evidence consistently points to the conclusion that differences in cognitive skills lead to significant differences in economic growth. Moreover, even if issues related to omitted factors or reverse causation remain, it seems very unlikely that these cause all of the estimated effects.[21]

Since the causality tests concentrate on the impact of schools, the evidence suggests that school policy, if effective in raising cognitive skills, can be an important force in economic development. While other factors – culture, health, and so forth – may affect the level of cognitive skills in an economy, schools clearly contribute to the development of human capital. More years of schooling in a system that is not well designed to enhance learning, however, will have little effect.

NOTES

1. See the reviews in Hanushek and Woessmann (2008), and OECD, Hanuskek and Woessmann (2010).

2. A major difference of perspective in modeling economic growth rests on whether education should be thought of as an input to overall production, affecting the level of income in a country but not the growth rate in the long run (augmented neoclassical models, as in Mankiw, Romer and Weil [1992]) or whether education directly affects the long-run growth rate (endogenous growth models as, importantly, in Lucas [1988], Romer [1990], and Aghion and Howitt [1998]). See Acemoglu (2009), Aghion and Howitt (2009), Barro and Sala-i-Martin (2004), and Jones and Vollrath (2013) for textbook introductions. In terms of these major theoretical distinctions, the formulation here combines key elements of both competing models. Because the model directly relates the rate of technological change and productivity improvement to the stock of a nation's human capital, it can be seen as an endogenous growth model. At the same time, by including the initial level of income among the control variables, the model does allow for conditional convergence, a leading feature of the augmented neoclassical approach. These alternatives in the projections of economic outcomes are examined in Chapter 5.

3. To give an idea of the robustness of this association, an extensive empirical analysis by Sala-i-Martin, Doppelhofer and Miller (2004) of 67 explanatory variables in growth regressions on a sample of 88 countries found that primary schooling was the most robust influence factor (after an East Asian dummy) on growth in per capita GDP in 1960-96.

4. Various analyses suggest that a difference in test scores of one-quarter to one-third of a standard deviation is equivalent to one year of school attainment. Thus, one way to characterise the differences in schooling between Korea and Brazil is to translate the approximately 1.5 standard deviation difference in PISA scores into differences in effective years of schooling for the 15-year-olds taking the PISA test: some 5-6 years difference in quality-equivalent years of schooling.

5. See Hanushek (1986, 2002) for reviews.

6. See Hanushek and Woessmann (2011) for a review. Note that there have been five major international assessments since 2003. Emphasis is placed on the early assessments because they fit into the analysis of long-run growth. The analysis of economic impacts for countries relies on the subsequent testing.

7. By transforming the means and variances of the original country scores (partly based on external longitudinal test score information available for the United States), each is placed into a common distribution of outcomes. Each age group and subject is normalised to the PISA standard of mean 500 and individual standard deviation of 100 across OECD countries, and then all available test scores are averaged at the country level.

8. The correlation between the measure based on student achievement tests between 1964 and 2003 and the recent adult numeracy achievement test of the Programme for the International Assessment of Adult Competencies (PIAAC), conducted in 2011/12, is 0.448 (statistically significant at the 6% level) among the 18 countries available in both data sets. Without three significant outliers (Korea doing better on the student tests, and Cyprus [see notes at the end of this Annex] and Norway doing better at the adult test), the correlation is 0.793 (significant at the 1% level).

9. For the 50 countries in the growth analysis, 73% of the variance in scores lies between countries (Hanushek and Woessmann [2012]). The remaining 27% includes both true score changes and any measurement error in the tests. Any measurement error in this case will tend to bias downward the estimates of the impact of cognitive skills on growth, so that the estimates of economic implications will be conservative.

10. For data on per capita GDP and its growth, the analyses used the Penn World Tables (Heston, Summers and Aten [2002]). Data on quantitative educational attainment are an extended version of the Cohen and Soto (2007) data. Results are very similar when using the latest Barro and Lee (2013) data on educational attainment; see Hanushek and Woessmann (2015), Appendix 3A.

11. See Hanushek and Woessmann (2012, 2015) for a more complete description of both the data and the estimation, which extends previous work by Hanushek and Kimko (2000).

12. To avoid the 2008 global recession, its aftermath, and any potential bubbles building up beforehand, the growth analysis stops in 2000, but results are very similar when extending the growth period to 2007 or 2009; see Hanushek and Woessmann (2015), Appendix 3A.

13. This section summarises the detailed analysis found in Hanushek and Woessmann (2015), Chapter 4.

14. See, for example, Bils and Klenow (2000).

15. See the review in Hanushek and Woessmann (2011).

16. See the extended discussion in Hanushek and Woessmann (2015), Chapter 4.

17. The formal approach is called "instrumental variables." In order for this to be a valid approach, it must be the case that the institutions are not themselves related to differences in growth beyond their relation with test scores. For a fuller discussion, see Hanushek and Woessmann (2012).

18. The formal approach is often called "difference-in-differences." Three potential problems arise in this analysis. First, it looks at the labour market returns just for the individual and not at the aggregate impact on the economy of achievement differences. Second, those who migrate at a young enough age to be educated in the United States might differ from those who migrate at later ages. Third, employers may treat people with a foreign education differently from those with a U.S. education. The second two potential problems, however, can affect the results only in complicated ways, because the identification of the impact of cognitive skills is based on a comparison across the home countries. As long as the impact of these is similar for the different origin countries, the results would remain. Any problems would come from different patterns of these factors that are correlated with test scores across countries.

19. Only 12 OECD countries have participated in international tests over a long enough period to provide the possibility of looking at trends in test performance over more than 30 years. The analysis simply considers a bivariate regression of test scores on time for countries with multiple observations. The trends in growth rates are determined in a similar manner: annual growth rates are regressed on a time trend. The analysis relates the slopes in the test regression to the slopes in the growth rate regression. Hanushek and Woessmann (2012) consider more complicated statistical relationships, but the overall results hold. They also hold when the sample of countries is expanded to include the non-OECD countries.

20. It is very unlikely that the changes in growth rates suffer the same reverse causality concerns suggested previously, because a change in growth rate can occur at varying income levels and varying rates of growth.

21. Another way to circumvent potential bias in cross-country regression estimates is to employ a development accounting framework that assumes a particular macroeconomic production function and takes parameter values from microeconometric earnings regressions. In such analyses, cognitive skills and years of schooling together play a major role in accounting for cross-country differences in current levels of per capita GDP (Hanushek and Woessmann, 2015, section 4.4). Such estimation is of course highly dependent on the choice of production function parameters. The development accounting in Hanushek and Woessmann (2015) relies on estimates for school attainment and cognitive skills from the International Adult Literacy Survey. Caselli (2014) employs much smaller estimates of the returns to cognitive skills and reaches different conclusions. His returns to skills come from a specific set of coefficient estimates in one Mexican study that uses a shortened-version of the Raven ability test to measure cognitive skills (Vogl, 2014), leading to questions of generalisability.

Notes regarding Cyprus

Readers should note the following information provided by Turkey and by the European Union Member States of the OECD and the European Union regarding the status of Cyprus:

Note by Turkey

The information in this document with reference to "Cyprus" relates to the southern part of the Island. There is no single authority representing both Turkish and Greek Cypriot people on the Island. Turkey recognises the Turkish Republic of Northern Cyprus (TRNC). Until a lasting and equitable solution is found within the context of the United Nations, Turkey shall preserve its position concerning the "Cyprus issue".

Note by all the European Union member States of the OECD and the European Union

The Republic of Cyprus is recognised by all members of the United Nations with the exception of Turkey. The information in this document relates to the area under the effective control of the Government of the Republic of Cyprus.

REFERENCES

Acemoglu, D. (2009), *Introduction to Modern Economic Growth*, Princeton University Press, Princeton, NJ.

Aghion, P. and P. Howitt (2009), *The Economics of Growth*, The MIT Press, Cambridge, MA.

Aghion, P. and P. Howitt (1998), *Endogenous Growth Theory*, The MIT Press, Cambridge, MA.

Barro, R.J. and J.W. Lee (2013), "A new data set of educational attainment in the world, 1950-2010", *Journal of Development Economics*, Vol. 104, pp. 184-198.

Barro, R.J. and X. Sala-i-Martin (2004), *Economic Growth*, second ed., The MIT Press, Cambridge, MA.

Bils, M. and P.J. Klenow (2000), "Does schooling cause growth?" *American Economic Review*, Vol. 90/5, pp. 1160-1183.

Caselli, F. (2014), "The Latin American efficiency gap", *CFM Discussion Paper*, Centre for Macroeconomics, London, pp. 2014-2021.

Cohen, D. and M. Soto (2007), "Growth and human capital: Good data, good results", *Journal of Economic Growth*, Vol. 12/1, pp. 51-76.

Hanushek, E.A. (2002), "Publicly provided education", in *Handbook of Public Economics*, Vol. 4, edited by A.J. Auerbach and M. Feldstein, Amsterdam, pp. 2045-2141.

Hanushek, E.A. (1986), "The economics of schooling: Production and efficiency in public schools", *Journal of Economic Literature*, Vol. 24/3, pp. 1141-1177.

Hanushek, E.A. and D.D. Kimko (2000), "Schooling, labor force quality, and the growth of nations", *American Economic Review*, Vol. 90/5, pp. 1184-1208.

Hanushek, E.A. and L. Woessmann (2015), *The Knowledge Capital of Nations: Education and the Economics of Growth*, The MIT Press, Cambridge, MA.

Hanushek, E.A. and L. Woessmann (2012), "Do better schools lead to more growth? Cognitive skills, economic outcomes, and causation", *Journal of Economic Growth*, Vol. 17/4, pp. 267-321.

Hanushek, E.A. and L. Woessmann (2011), "The economics of international differences in educational achievement", in E.A. Hanushek, S. Machin and L. Woessmann (eds), *Handbook of the Economics of Education*, Vol. 3, Amsterdam, pp. 89-200.

Hanushek, E.A. and L. Woessmann (2008), "The role of cognitive skills in economic development", *Journal of Economic Literature*, Vol. 46/3, pp. 607-668.

Heston, Alan, Robert Summers and Bettina Aten (2002), "Penn World Table Version 6.1", Center for International Comparisons at the University of Pennsylvania (CICUP), University of Pennsylvania, Philadelphia, PA.

Jones, C.I. and D. Vollrath (2013), *Introduction to Economic Growth*, third ed., W.W. Norton and Company, New York, NY.

Lucas, R.E. Jr. (1988), "On the mechanics of economic development", *Journal of Monetary Economics*, Vol. 22/1, pp. 3-42.

Mankiw, N.G., D. Romer and D. Weil (1992), "A contribution to the empirics of economic growth", *Quarterly Journal of Economics*, Vol. 107/2, pp. 407-437.

OECD, E.A. Hanushek and L. Woessmann (2010), *The High Cost of Low Educational Performance: The Long-run Economic Impact of Improving PISA Outcomes*, OECD Publishing, Paris, http://dx.doi.org/10.1787/9789264077485-en.

Romer, P. (1990), "Endogenous technological change", *Journal of Political Economy*, Vol. 99/5, pt. II, pp. S71-S102.

Sala-i-Martin, X., G. Doppelhofer and R.I. Miller (2004), "Determinants of long-term growth: A Bayesian Averaging of Classical Estimates (BACE) approach", *American Economic Review*, Vol. 94/4, pp. 813-835.

Vogl, T.S. (2014), "Height, skills, and labor market outcomes in Mexico", *Journal of Development Economics*, Vol. 107, pp. 84-96.

Annex B

Transforming performance in TIMSS onto the PISA scale

The data on educational achievement generally refer to the average of mathematics and science achievement on the PISA (Programme for International Student Assessment) 2012 test. Data on country mean achievement are derived from OECD (2013). Data on shares of students below specific achievement levels are calculated from the underlying PISA micro database (which does not contain data for Cyprus; see notes at the end of this Annex). A total of 65 countries participated in PISA 2012, 62 of which have the internationally comparable economic data necessary to be included in the projection analyses.

An additional 16 countries that did not participate in the PISA 2012 test participated in the 8th-grade 2011 TIMSS (Trends in International Mathematics and Science Study) test, 14 with internationally comparable economic data (see Mullis et al. [2012]; Martin et al. [2012]). A total of 28 countries participated in both the PISA and the TIMSS tests.[1] Among these 28 countries, the correlation of average achievement scores across the two tests is 0.944 in math and 0.930 in science. These high levels of conformity warrant a joint consideration of performance on these two international tests.

The following method is used to derive measures of educational achievement comparable to the PISA scale for the 16 countries that did not participate in PISA but did participate in TIMSS. TIMSS data are rescaled so that the group of 28 countries that participated in both PISA 2012 and TIMSS 2011 has the same mean and standard deviation at the student level as on the PISA test. (A smooth normal shape of the student-level test score data in this group of countries on both tests suggests that such a re-scaling procedure is warranted). From this re-scaling, educational achievement data on the PISA scale are derived for the 16 countries, which allows for calculating the required means and shares of educational achievement.

Deviating from the TIMSS sampling directives, which required the sampling of students in 8th grade, three countries sampled students in 9th grade ("out-of-grade participants"): Botswana, South Africa and Honduras. The TIMSS International Study Center encourages this approach in countries where the TIMSS 8th-grade assessment is deemed too difficult for 8th-grade students (see Mullis et al. [2012], p. 38).

Table B.1 provides complete test information for the 76-country sample along with an indicator for whether the data come from PISA or TIMSS. Countries are divided into income groups based on their per capita GDP.

Table B.2 provides test information for the five countries that did not have internationally comparable economic data.

TABLE B.1 COUNTRY PERFORMANCE, ENROLMENT RATES, INCOME AND POPULATION

Countries/Economies that participated in PISA and/or TIMSS

	Average score	Mathematics score	Science score	Share below 420 points	Increased score	Mathematics boys	Science boys	Mathematics girls	Science girls	25th percentile	PISA	Enrolment rate	Per capita GDP	GDP	Population
Lower-middle income countries															
Armenia	428.1	445.5	410.7	0.447	463.7	440.8	401.2	450.4	420.8	363.3	0	0.87	7 748	26	3.3
Georgia	401.4	410.0	392.7	0.549	451.4	411.4	387.6	408.6	398.5	333.5	0	0.81	8 223	37	4.5
Ghana	290.8	309.7	271.9	0.892	424.9	320.9	286.9	297.4	255.3	218.8	0	0.46	4 338	117	26.9
Honduras	327.7	316.9	338.5	0.872	425.6	329.7	350.5	306.5	328.7	272.3	0	0.74	4 849	41	8.4
Indonesia	378.5	375.1	381.9	0.738	432.4	377.4	380.4	372.8	383.5	331.2	1	0.86	10 759	2 744	255.1
Morocco	348.0	350.1	346.0	0.789	430.8	350.1	344.3	350.0	348.0	287.0	0	0.79	8 097	271	33.5
Ukraine	468.4	458.1	478.7	0.283	485.8	459.7	480.9	456.5	476.5	411.2	0	0.85	8 494	384	45.2
Viet Nam	519.9	511.3	528.4	0.113	524.6	516.6	529.0	506.7	527.9	466.3	1	0.64	5 983	548	91.6
Upper-middle income countries															
Albania	395.9	394.3	397.4	0.591	446.0	394.0	393.9	394.7	401.1	338.9	1	0.65	11 689	32	2.8
Argentina	397.0	388.4	405.6	0.611	442.3	395.6	402.2	381.7	408.9	343.4	1	0.93	21 924	930	42.4
Botswana	375.9	375.6	376.3	0.670	438.7	368.5	370.5	382.2	381.8	314.2	0	0.60	16 758	36	2.1
Brazil	398.1	391.5	404.7	0.643	441.0	400.8	405.5	382.9	403.9	341.1	1	0.78	15 519	3 173	204.5
Bulgaria	442.6	438.7	446.5	0.420	471.9	437.6	436.7	440.0	456.9	373.0	1	0.85	17 869	128	7.2
Colombia	387.6	376.5	398.7	0.676	437.2	390.0	408.0	364.5	390.4	336.6	1	0.70	14 164	683	48.2
Costa Rica	418.2	407.0	429.4	0.525	447.0	419.5	435.6	395.9	423.8	371.1	1	0.79	15 534	75	4.8
Hungary	485.7	477.0	494.3	0.245	498.8	481.7	495.9	472.7	492.8	421.5	1	0.97	25 406	250	9.8
Iran	422.2	393.9	450.5	0.498	461.1	397.0	447.9	390.2	453.5	355.9	0	0.74	16 918	1 336	79.0
Jordan	397.5	385.6	409.4	0.614	442.3	375.1	387.8	395.8	430.4	344.8	1	0.97	12 398	85	6.8
Kazakhstan	428.3	431.8	424.7	0.463	453.2	432.0	420.4	431.6	429.0	378.6	1	0.95	25 367	449	17.7
Lebanon	403.1	428.2	378.0	0.553	449.2	434.9	380.3	422.7	376.1	339.9	0	0.75	18 358	84	4.6
Macedonia	392.3	405.0	379.5	0.570	453.8	401.7	370.3	408.6	389.2	312.6	0	0.78	13 901	29	2.1
Malaysia	420.0	420.5	419.5	0.511	452.1	416.5	413.8	424.3	424.9	363.7	1	0.84	25 833	800	31.0
Mexico	414.1	413.3	414.9	0.538	446.0	420.4	418.1	406.4	411.8	365.4	1	0.70	18 714	2 260	120.8
Montenegro	409.9	409.6	410.1	0.560	448.8	409.7	401.7	409.6	418.5	352.2	1	1.00	15 996	10	0.6
Peru	370.6	368.1	373.1	0.737	434.0	377.8	376.1	358.9	370.3	315.5	1	0.87	12 639	403	31.9
Romania	441.7	444.6	438.8	0.416	463.6	446.5	436.2	442.7	441.3	384.4	1	1.00	20 356	404	19.8
Serbia	446.8	448.9	444.8	0.391	470.3	453.5	442.7	444.3	446.9	385.6	1	0.95	12 971	93	7.2
South Africa	314.9	330.8	299.0	0.856	430.8	329.2	295.6	332.6	302.8	242.6	0	0.72	13 078	712	54.4
Thailand	435.4	426.7	444.0	0.442	459.5	419.1	433.2	432.7	452.5	381.9	1	0.80	15 320	1 055	68.9
Tunisia	392.9	387.8	398.0	0.639	439.8	395.9	398.6	380.7	397.6	339.2	1	1.00	11 897	132	11.1
Turkey	455.7	448.0	463.4	0.364	474.4	451.9	458.3	443.9	468.6	394.3	1	0.76	20 299	1 586	78.2
High-income non-OECD countries															
Bahrain	407.7	388.1	427.2	0.534	456.9	366.8	396.0	409.7	458.7	336.1	0	0.89	52 830	65	1.2
Croatia	481.2	471.1	491.4	0.251	493.6	476.8	490.2	465.2	492.5	420.3	1	0.97	20 873	89	4.3
Cyprus*	438.7	439.7	437.7			439.9	431.4	439.5	444.1		1	1.00	28 329	26	0.9
Hong Kong-China	558.1	561.2	554.9	0.075	561.8	568.4	558.0	553.0	551.4	501.9	1	0.92	57 677	421	7.3
Latvia	496.4	490.6	502.2	0.174	503.8	488.7	494.5	492.5	510.0	441.4	1	0.98	25 195	51	2.0
Lithuania	487.3	478.8	495.7	0.225	498.7	478.9	488.3	478.7	503.2	428.0	1	0.92	28 245	83	2.9
Oman	368.8	345.1	392.6	0.650	445.1	313.1	350.5	375.7	433.0	290.4	0	0.82	44 904	172	3.8
Qatar	380.0	376.4	383.6	0.677	445.8	368.7	366.8	384.7	401.6	307.7	1	0.99	146 012	355	2.4
Russian Federation	484.2	482.2	486.3	0.230	495.4	481.4	483.5	482.9	489.1	425.3	1	1.00	25 351	3 643	143.7
Saudi Arabia	391.4	372.7	410.1	0.612	444.5	365.6	396.8	380.4	424.3	330.2	0	0.72	56 253	1 757	31.2
Singapore	562.5	573.5	551.5	0.098	567.3	571.9	551.2	575.1	551.8	490.3	1	0.97	84 821	467	5.5
Chinese Taipei	541.6	559.8	523.3	0.123	547.7	562.5	523.8	557.2	522.8	473.5	1	1.00	45 997	1 080	23.5
United Arab Emirates	441.2	434.0	448.4	0.427	468.3	431.5	434.1	436.4	462.0	376.0	1	0.99	67 202	644	9.6
Uruguay	412.6	409.3	415.8	0.536	453.4	415.4	415.3	403.9	416.3	349.7	1	0.85	21 387	73	3.4

TABLE B.1 COUNTRY PERFORMANCE, ENROLMENT RATES, INCOME AND POPULATION (continued)

Countries/Economies that participated in PISA and/or TIMSS

	Average score	Mathematics score	Science score	Share below 420 points	Increased score	Mathematics boys	Science boys	Mathematics girls	Science girls	25th percentile	PISA	Enrolment rate	Per capita GDP	GDP	Population
High-income OECD countries															
Australia	512.8	504.2	521.5	0.177	522.1	510.1	523.7	497.8	519.1	445.2	1	0.99	48 288	1 153	23.9
Austria	505.7	505.5	505.8	0.185	514.9	516.7	510.1	494.5	501.5	441.0	1	0.95	46 906	401	8.6
Belgium	509.7	514.5	504.9	0.196	521.5	520.1	506.8	508.9	502.9	441.0	1	0.98	42 923	482	11.2
Canada	521.8	518.1	525.4	0.131	528.0	523.1	526.9	513.0	524.0	462.0	1	0.98	45 982	1 647	35.8
Chile	433.8	422.6	444.9	0.453	459.9	435.5	448.4	410.5	441.6	376.6	1	0.92	24 170	432	17.9
Czech Republic	503.6	499.0	508.3	0.187	513.4	504.7	508.7	492.9	507.9	440.4	1	0.96	29 659	313	10.6
Denmark	499.3	500.0	498.5	0.181	508.5	507.0	503.5	493.0	493.4	441.0	1	0.98	45 800	258	5.6
Estonia	531.0	520.5	541.4	0.085	534.1	523.2	540.2	517.9	542.6	475.9	1	0.98	27 729	37	1.3
Finland	532.1	518.8	545.4	0.107	537.3	517.4	537.4	520.2	553.9	474.3	1	0.99	41 394	228	5.5
France	497.0	495.0	499.0	0.218	510.3	499.4	497.7	490.9	500.2	431.0	1	0.95	41 396	2 659	64.2
Germany	518.8	513.5	524.1	0.161	527.2	520.2	523.9	506.6	524.4	454.1	1	1.00	46 166	3 742	81.1
Greece	459.8	453.0	466.7	0.325	479.1	457.0	460.0	449.0	473.3	400.3	1	0.95	27 008	298	11.0
Iceland	485.5	492.8	478.2	0.244	500.2	489.7	476.7	495.9	479.7	422.2	1	1.00	44 575	14	0.3
Ireland	511.8	501.5	522.0	0.151	519.1	509.0	523.9	493.7	520.0	453.7	1	0.98	48 787	236	4.8
Israel*	468.3	466.5	470.1	0.327	491.8	472.4	469.7	460.7	470.4	394.2	1	0.95	34 162	281	8.2
Italy	489.4	485.3	493.5	0.232	502.1	494.2	494.9	475.8	492.1	425.8	1	0.94	35 228	2 122	60.2
Japan	541.6	536.4	546.7	0.104	546.9	544.9	551.9	527.0	541.0	479.2	1	0.98	38 797	4 917	126.7
Korea	545.8	553.8	537.8	0.086	549.8	562.1	539.4	544.2	535.9	485.6	1	0.98	37 413	1 895	50.7
Luxembourg	490.5	489.8	491.2	0.247	505.0	502.2	498.7	477.1	483.5	420.5	1	0.98	94 167	53	0.6
Netherlands	522.5	523.0	522.1	0.151	529.9	528.0	523.6	517.7	520.4	457.9	1	1.00	48 798	824	16.9
New Zealand	507.7	499.7	515.6	0.207	519.0	507.1	517.9	492.1	513.3	436.0	1	0.97	36 343	166	4.6
Norway	491.9	489.4	494.5	0.223	504.7	490.4	492.8	488.3	496.3	428.4	1	1.00	67 619	352	5.2
Poland	521.7	517.5	525.8	0.127	526.9	519.6	524.4	515.5	527.1	460.4	1	0.96	25 703	991	38.5
Portugal	488.2	487.1	489.3	0.233	500.9	492.7	488.3	481.3	490.2	425.3	1	1.00	27 180	285	10.5
Slovak Republic	476.4	481.6	471.2	0.288	495.1	486.1	474.7	476.7	467.4	407.9	1	0.99	28 888	157	5.4
Slovenia	507.6	501.1	514.1	0.177	515.7	502.7	509.9	499.4	518.7	442.3	1	0.97	30 266	63	2.1
Spain	490.4	484.3	496.4	0.211	501.3	492.4	500.1	476.0	492.7	431.9	1	0.95	34 229	1 588	46.4
Sweden	481.5	478.3	484.8	0.261	497.1	476.9	481.2	479.6	488.5	417.1	1	1.00	46 386	454	9.8
Switzerland	523.1	530.9	515.3	0.138	529.9	537.4	518.3	524.5	512.3	460.5	1	0.98	56 816	460	8.1
United Kingdom	504.0	493.9	514.1	0.196	515.0	500.3	520.6	487.8	507.9	438.7	1	1.00	39 225	2 547	64.9
United States	489.4	481.4	497.4	0.235	501.1	483.6	496.5	479.0	498.3	424.5	1	1.00	57 045	18 287	320.6

* See notes at the end of this Annex.

Notes:

Average/mathematics/science score: Average mathematics/science score on international student achievement test. PISA participants: PISA 2012 score; TIMSS (non-PISA) participants: based on 8th-grade TIMSS 2011 micro data, transformed to PISA scale. See Annex B for details.

Share below 420 points: Share of students performing below 420 points on international student achievement test. Average of mathematics and science. See Annex B for details.

Increased score: Average achievement after all students performing below 420 points are lifted to 420 points. Average of mathematics and science.

Mathematics/science boys/girls: Average achievement score of boys and girls, respectively, in the respective subject.

25th percentile: Score at the 25th percentile of the distribution on international student achievement test. Average of mathematics and science. See Annex B for details.

PISA: 1 = PISA participant; 0 = TIMSS (non-PISA) participant.

Enrolment rate: PISA participants: Share of 15-year-olds enrolled in school; TIMSS (non-PISA) participants: Net enrolment ratio in secondary education (% of relevant group).

Per capita GDP: Gross domestic product per capita based on purchasing-power-parity (PPP, current international dollar), IMF estimate, 2015.

GDP: Gross domestic product based on purchasing-power-parity (PPP, current international dollar), IMF estimate, 2015 (in billions).

Population: Persons (in millions).

TABLE B.2 PERFORMANCE OF COUNTRIES THAT LACK INTERNATIONALLY COMPARABLE GDP DATA

	Average score	Mathematics score	Science score	Share below 420 points
PISA participants				
Liechtenstein	529.8	535.0	524.7	0.137
Macao-China	529.4	538.1	520.6	0.107
Shanghai-China	596.4	612.7	580.1	0.036
TIMSS participants				
Palestine	388.2	383.1	393.3	0.599
Syria	379.3	359.1	399.6	0.646

Notes: See Table B.1.

NOTES

1. The 28 countries participating both in PISA 2012 and in eighth-grade TIMSS 2011 are Australia, Chile, Finland, Hong Kong-China, Hungary, Indonesia, Israel, Italy, Japan, Jordan, Kazakhstan, Korea, Lithuania, Malaysia, New Zealand, Norway, Qatar, Romania, the Russian Federation, Singapore, Slovenia, Sweden, Chinese Taipei, Thailand, Tunisia, Turkey, the United Arab Emirates and the United States.

Notes regarding Cyprus

Readers should note the following information provided by Turkey and by the European Union Member States of the OECD and the European Union regarding the status of Cyprus:

Note by Turkey

The information in this document with reference to "Cyprus" relates to the southern part of the Island. There is no single authority representing both Turkish and Greek Cypriot people on the Island. Turkey recognises the Turkish Republic of Northern Cyprus (TRNC). Until a lasting and equitable solution is found within the context of the United Nations, Turkey shall preserve its position concerning the "Cyprus issue".

Note by all the European Union member States of the OECD and the European Union

The Republic of Cyprus is recognised by all members of the United Nations with the exception of Turkey. The information in this document relates to the area under the effective control of the Government of the Republic of Cyprus.

Note regarding Israel

The statistical data for Israel are supplied by and under the responsibility of the relevant Israeli authorities. The use of such data by the OECD is without prejudice to the status of the Golan Heights, East Jerusalem and Israeli settlements in the West Bank under the terms of international law.

REFERENCES

Martin, M.O. et al. (2012), *TIMSS 2011 International Results in Science*, TIMSS and PIRLS International Study Center, Boston College, Chestnut Hill, MA.

Mullis, I.V.S. et al. (2012), *TIMSS 2011 Encyclopedia: Education Policy and Curriculum in Mathematics and Science*, Volumes 1 and 2, TIMSS and PIRLS International Study Center, Boston College, Chestnut Hill, MA .

OECD (2014), *PISA 2012 Results: What Students Know and Can Do (Volume I, Revised edition, February 2014): Student Performance in Mathematics, Reading and Science*, PISA, OECD Publishing, Paris, http://dx.doi.org/10.1787/9789264208780-en.

Annex C

Augmented neoclassical results

Table C.1 provides country details on each policy scenario when the projections employ a neoclassical growth model.

TABLE C.1 LOWER-BOUND PROJECTION RESULTS FROM AUGMENTED NEOCLASSICAL MODEL SPECIFICATION

	25 PISA point increase			Gender equality			Scenario I: All current students acquire basic skills			Scenario II: Full enrolment at current quality			Scenario III: Universal basic skills			Scenario IV: 30-year improvement		
	Value of reform (bn USD)	In % of current GDP	In % of discounted future GDP	Value of reform (bn USD)	In % of current GDP	In % of discounted future GDP	Value of reform (bn USD)	In % of current GDP	In % of discounted future GDP	Value of reform (bn USD)	In % of current GDP	In % of discounted future GDP	Value of reform (bn USD)	In % of current GDP	In % of discounted future GDP	Value of reform (bn USD)	In % of current GDP	In % of discounted future GDP
Lower-middle income countries																		
Armenia	69	268%	5.6%	20	77%	1.6%	100	391%	8.1%	26	100%	2.1%	130	509%	10.5%	98	384%	7.9%
Georgia	71	193%	4.7%	6	16%	0.4%	149	408%	9.8%	44	121%	2.9%	219	599%	14.4%	163	445%	10.7%
Ghana	63	54%	1.9%	32	28%	1.0%	382	327%	11.6%	228	195%	6.9%	1 415	1213%	43.0%	980	840%	29.8%
Honduras	47	115%	3.5%	23	56%	1.7%	210	514%	15.8%	37	90%	2.8%	359	877%	27.0%	257	629%	19.3%
Indonesia	4 225	154%	4.4%	61	2%	0.1%	9 699	353%	10.1%	1 229	45%	1.3%	12 639	461%	13.2%	9 290	338%	9.7%
Morocco	328	121%	3.8%	12	5%	0.1%	1 217	448%	13.9%	209	77%	2.4%	1 869	689%	21.4%	1 348	497%	15.4%
Ukraine	1 374	358%	6.1%	100	26%	0.4%	941	245%	4.2%	536	140%	2.4%	1 520	396%	6.7%	1 163	303%	5.1%
Viet Nam	2 608	476%	5.4%	294	54%	0.6%	476	87%	1.0%	3 243	592%	6.7%	3 773	689%	7.8%	2 931	535%	6.1%
Upper-middle income countries																		
Albania	42	129%	3.5%	3	10%	0.3%	87	269%	7.2%	51	158%	4.2%	174	540%	14.5%	128	398%	10.7%
Argentina	1 392	150%	4.5%	97	10%	0.3%	2 645	284%	8.6%	211	23%	0.7%	3 016	324%	9.9%	2 218	238%	7.2%
Botswana	31	88%	2.8%	7	21%	0.7%	83	232%	7.4%	53	148%	4.7%	196	550%	17.4%	142	399%	12.6%
Brazil	4 517	142%	4.0%	882	28%	0.8%	8 035	253%	7.1%	2 868	90%	2.5%	12 772	403%	11.3%	9 424	297%	8.4%
Bulgaria	276	216%	5.0%	62	49%	1.1%	327	256%	6.0%	132	103%	2.4%	477	372%	8.7%	357	279%	6.5%
Colombia	820	120%	3.5%	365	53%	1.6%	1 698	249%	7.2%	723	106%	3.1%	3 133	459%	13.3%	2 300	337%	9.8%
Costa Rica	128	171%	4.4%	47	62%	1.6%	149	199%	5.1%	63	84%	2.1%	223	296%	7.6%	166	221%	5.7%
Hungary	788	315%	6.4%	94	38%	0.8%	400	160%	3.2%	52	21%	0.4%	455	182%	3.7%	347	139%	2.8%
Iran	2 137	160%	4.1%	22	2%	0.0%	3 420	256%	6.5%	1 985	149%	3.8%	5 712	428%	10.9%	4 246	318%	8.1%
Jordan	164	194%	5.2%	100	118%	3.2%	309	364%	9.8%	11	13%	0.3%	328	387%	10.4%	243	287%	7.7%
Kazakhstan	849	189%	5.1%	65	14%	0.4%	849	189%	5.1%	75	17%	0.5%	933	208%	5.6%	697	155%	4.2%
Lebanon	112	134%	3.8%	19	23%	0.7%	215	257%	7.3%	94	112%	3.2%	357	427%	12.2%	263	314%	9.0%
Macedonia	41	141%	4.0%	10	36%	1.0%	107	371%	10.5%	37	129%	3.6%	172	595%	16.8%	126	435%	12.3%
Malaysia	1 228	153%	4.3%	215	27%	0.8%	1 599	200%	5.6%	506	63%	1.8%	2 176	272%	7.7%	1 614	202%	5.7%
Mexico	3 053	135%	3.7%	610	27%	0.7%	3 941	174%	4.7%	2 578	114%	3.1%	7 178	318%	8.6%	5 332	236%	6.4%
Montenegro	20	202%	5.4%	3	32%	0.9%	33	326%	8.7%	0	0%	0.0%	33	326%	8.7%	24	243%	6.5%
Peru	553	137%	4.2%	136	34%	1.0%	1 525	378%	11.6%	174	43%	1.3%	1 964	487%	14.9%	1 432	355%	10.9%
Romania	976	242%	5.8%	11	3%	0.1%	852	211%	5.1%	0	0%	0.0%	852	211%	5.1%	641	159%	3.8%
Serbia	265	283%	6.0%	13	14%	0.3%	247	265%	5.6%	34	37%	0.8%	286	306%	6.5%	216	231%	4.9%
South Africa	500	70%	2.8%	54	8%	0.3%	2 710	381%	15.0%	565	79%	3.1%	4 923	692%	27.2%	3 441	483%	19.0%
Thailand	2 125	201%	4.7%	593	56%	1.3%	2 047	194%	4.5%	1 115	106%	2.5%	3 276	310%	7.2%	2 462	233%	5.4%
Tunisia	259	196%	5.3%	43	32%	0.9%	513	388%	10.6%	0	0%	0.0%	513	388%	10.6%	380	287%	7.8%
Turkey	3 253	205%	4.6%	73	5%	0.1%	2 399	151%	3.4%	2 461	155%	3.5%	5 044	318%	7.1%	3 800	240%	5.4%
High-income non-OECD countries																		
Bahrain	73	113%	3.9%	78	120%	4.1%	151	234%	8.1%	25	39%	1.3%	187	290%	10.0%	136	211%	7.3%
Croatia	290	325%	6.4%	25	28%	0.5%	139	156%	3.1%	23	26%	0.5%	164	183%	3.6%	125	140%	2.8%
Cyprus*	53	208%	5.5%	6	25%	0.7%				0	0%	0.0%						
Hong Kong-China	1 722	409%	6.7%	333	79%	1.3%	241	57%	0.9%	299	71%	1.2%	546	130%	2.1%	420	100%	1.6%

TABLE C.1 LOWER-BOUND PROJECTION RESULTS FROM AUGMENTED NEOCLASSICAL MODEL SPECIFICATION (continued)

	25 PISA point increase			Gender equality			Scenario I: All current students acquire basic skills			Scenario II: Full enrolment at current quality			Scenario III: Universal basic skills			Scenario IV: 30-year improvement		
	Value of reform (bn USD)	In % of current GDP	In % of discounted future GDP	Value of reform (bn USD)	In % of current GDP	In % of discounted future GDP	Value of reform (bn USD)	In % of current GDP	In % of discounted future GDP	Value of reform (bn USD)	In % of current GDP	In % of discounted future GDP	Value of reform (bn USD)	In % of current GDP	In % of discounted future GDP	Value of reform (bn USD)	In % of current GDP	In % of discounted future GDP
Latvia	178	349%	6.6%	33	65%	1.2%	51	99%	1.9%	8	16%	0.3%	59	116%	2.2%	45	89%	1.7%
Lithuania	241	290%	5.9%	34	41%	0.8%	107	129%	2.6%	45	55%	1.1%	155	186%	3.8%	118	142%	2.9%
Oman	138	80%	3.2%	200	116%	4.6%	464	269%	10.6%	94	54%	2.1%	676	392%	15.5%	481	279%	11.0%
Qatar	248	70%	3.2%	127	36%	1.7%	715	202%	9.3%	8	2%	0.1%	732	206%	9.6%	518	146%	6.8%
Russian Federation	11 647	320%	6.5%	776	21%	0.4%	5 041	138%	2.8%	77	2%	0.0%	5 123	141%	2.9%	3 904	107%	2.2%
Saudi Arabia	1 360	77%	2.9%	580	33%	1.2%	3 027	172%	6.4%	1 293	74%	2.8%	5 335	304%	11.4%	3 845	219%	8.2%
Singapore	1 803	386%	6.8%	67	14%	0.3%	332	71%	1.3%	139	30%	0.5%	474	102%	1.8%	364	78%	1.4%
Chinese Taipei	4 533	420%	7.2%	272	25%	0.4%	1 060	98%	1.7%	1	0%	0.0%	1 061	98%	1.7%	817	76%	1.3%
United Arab Emirates	985	153%	4.8%	304	47%	1.5%	1 074	167%	5.2%	19	3%	0.1%	1 095	170%	5.3%	810	126%	3.9%
Uruguay	114	156%	4.4%	12	16%	0.5%	193	264%	7.4%	49	67%	1.9%	258	354%	9.9%	191	261%	7.3%
High-income OECD countries																		
Australia	3 650	316%	6.4%	567	49%	1.0%	1 303	113%	2.3%	123	11%	0.2%	1 431	124%	2.5%	1 091	95%	1.9%
Austria	1 162	290%	6.1%	345	86%	1.8%	415	103%	2.2%	143	36%	0.7%	565	141%	2.9%	429	107%	2.2%
Belgium	1 549	321%	6.4%	220	46%	0.9%	706	146%	2.9%	65	14%	0.3%	775	161%	3.2%	591	122%	2.5%
Canada	5 695	346%	6.6%	698	42%	0.8%	1 350	82%	1.6%	263	16%	0.3%	1 622	98%	1.9%	1 241	75%	1.4%
Chile	838	194%	5.1%	265	61%	1.6%	878	203%	5.3%	160	37%	1.0%	1 058	245%	6.4%	791	183%	4.8%
Czech Republic	1 072	343%	6.5%	125	40%	0.8%	403	129%	2.4%	103	33%	0.6%	511	163%	3.1%	390	125%	2.4%
Denmark	735	285%	6.1%	168	65%	1.4%	261	101%	2.2%	33	13%	0.3%	296	115%	2.5%	225	87%	1.9%
Estonia	169	457%	7.3%	5	12%	0.2%	20	54%	0.9%	6	16%	0.3%	26	70%	1.1%	20	54%	0.9%
Finland	911	400%	7.0%	171	75%	1.3%	179	79%	1.4%	10	5%	0.1%	190	83%	1.5%	146	64%	1.1%
France	7 499	282%	6.0%	441	17%	0.4%	3 883	146%	3.1%	932	35%	0.7%	4 878	183%	3.9%	3 702	139%	3.0%
Germany	12 867	344%	6.7%	1 557	42%	0.8%	4 109	110%	2.1%	0	0%	0.0%	4 109	110%	2.1%	3 141	84%	1.6%
Greece	717	241%	5.6%	35	12%	0.3%	543	182%	4.3%	84	28%	0.7%	635	213%	5.0%	479	161%	3.8%
Iceland	38	261%	6.0%	3	23%	0.5%	22	150%	3.4%	0	2%	0.0%	22	152%	3.5%	17	115%	2.6%
Ireland	729	309%	6.3%	131	56%	1.1%	204	86%	1.8%	36	15%	0.3%	241	102%	2.1%	184	78%	1.6%
Israel*	666	237%	5.6%	70	25%	0.6%	623	222%	5.2%	94	33%	0.8%	728	259%	6.1%	548	195%	4.6%
Italy	5 855	276%	5.9%	1 142	54%	1.1%	2 885	136%	2.9%	963	45%	1.0%	3 908	184%	3.9%	2 966	140%	3.0%
Japan	21 525	438%	7.2%	5 621	114%	1.9%	4 332	88%	1.4%	1 123	23%	0.4%	5 486	112%	1.8%	4 229	86%	1.4%
Korea	8 729	461%	7.3%	1 651	87%	1.4%	1 343	71%	1.1%	441	23%	0.4%	1 794	95%	1.5%	1 385	73%	1.2%
Luxembourg	106	202%	5.4%	41	77%	2.0%	60	114%	3.0%	5	9%	0.2%	65	124%	3.3%	49	93%	2.5%
Netherlands	2 853	346%	6.7%	354	43%	0.8%	801	97%	1.9%	29	4%	0.1%	831	101%	1.9%	636	77%	1.5%
New Zealand	551	331%	6.5%	101	60%	1.2%	241	145%	2.8%	46	28%	0.5%	290	174%	3.4%	221	133%	2.6%
Norway	830	236%	5.8%	12	3%	0.1%	412	117%	2.9%	4	1%	0.0%	416	118%	2.9%	314	89%	2.2%
Poland	4 211	425%	7.0%	53	5%	0.1%	837	85%	1.4%	353	36%	0.6%	1 200	121%	2.0%	924	93%	1.5%
Portugal	922	323%	6.5%	82	29%	0.6%	453	159%	3.2%	0	0%	0.0%	453	159%	3.2%	345	121%	2.4%
Slovak Republic	444	283%	6.2%	67	43%	0.9%	327	208%	4.5%	7	4%	0.1%	334	213%	4.7%	253	161%	3.5%
Slovenia	223	356%	6.6%	12	19%	0.4%	68	109%	2.0%	16	25%	0.5%	85	135%	2.5%	65	104%	1.9%
Spain	4 561	287%	6.1%	1 025	65%	1.4%	1 928	121%	2.6%	476	30%	0.6%	2 431	153%	3.2%	1 848	116%	2.5%
Sweden	1 131	249%	5.9%	109	24%	0.6%	686	151%	3.6%	2	0%	0.0%	687	151%	3.6%	519	114%	2.7%
Switzerland	1 480	322%	6.4%	264	57%	1.1%	386	84%	1.7%	80	17%	0.3%	469	102%	2.0%	358	78%	1.6%
United Kingdom	8 203	322%	6.5%	2 010	79%	1.6%	3 485	137%	2.8%	0	0%	0.0%	3 485	137%	2.8%	2 656	104%	2.1%
United States	45 048	246%	5.9%	1 186	6%	0.2%	20 405	112%	2.7%	0	0%	0.0%	20 405	112%	2.7%	15 419	84%	2.0%

* See notes at the end of this Annex.

Notes: Discounted value of future increases in GDP until 2095 due to the respective reform, expressed in billion U.S. dollars (PPP), as a percentage of current GDP, and as a percentage of discounted future GDP. See text for reform parameters.

PISA stands for the Programme for International Student Assessment.

NOTES

Notes regarding Cyprus

Readers should note the following information provided by Turkey and by the European Union Member States of the OECD and the European Union regarding the status of Cyprus:

Note by Turkey

The information in this document with reference to "Cyprus" relates to the southern part of the Island. There is no single authority representing both Turkish and Greek Cypriot people on the Island. Turkey recognises the Turkish Republic of Northern Cyprus (TRNC). Until a lasting and equitable solution is found within the context of the United Nations, Turkey shall preserve its position concerning the "Cyprus issue".

Note by all the European Union member States of the OECD and the European Union

The Republic of Cyprus is recognised by all members of the United Nations with the exception of Turkey. The information in this document relates to the area under the effective control of the Government of the Republic of Cyprus.

Note regarding Israel

The statistical data for Israel are supplied by and under the responsibility of the relevant Israeli authorities. The use of such data by the OECD is without prejudice to the status of the Golan Heights, East Jerusalem and Israeli settlements in the West Bank under the terms of international law.

Annex D

Distribution of skills when goal of universal basic skills is achieved

Table D.1 provides information on how the achievement of universal basic skills alters the mean and standard deviation of skills for countries with universal access to secondary schools.

TABLE D.1 MEANS AND STANDARD DEVIATIONS OF PERFORMANCE, BEFORE AND AFTER ATTAINING UNIVERSAL BASIC SKILLS

	Baseline average achievement	Baseline within-country standard deviation	Post-reform average achievement	Post-reform within-country standard deviation	Achievement gain	Standard deviation reduction
Australia	512.8	98.3	522.1	83.8	9.3	14.5
Belgium	509.7	101.7	521.5	83.1	11.8	18.6
Canada	521.8	89.9	528.0	79.3	6.2	10.7
Denmark	499.3	87.4	508.5	72.8	9.2	14.6
Estonia	531.0	80.5	534.1	74.8	3.1	5.7
Finland	532.1	89.1	537.3	79.6	5.2	9.6
Germany	518.8	95.7	527.2	81.9	8.3	13.8
Iceland	485.5	95.7	500.2	74.5	14.7	21.1
Ireland	511.8	88.0	519.1	75.8	7.3	12.2
Japan	541.6	94.5	546.9	84.6	5.3	10.0
Korea	545.8	90.5	549.8	82.5	4.1	8.0
Latvia	496.4	80.3	503.8	68.7	7.4	11.6
Luxembourg	490.5	99.3	505.0	79.0	14.5	20.3
Montenegro	409.9	83.6	448.8	46.5	39.0	37.1
Netherlands	522.5	93.4	529.9	81.1	7.4	12.3
Norway	491.9	95.1	504.7	75.9	12.8	19.2
Portugal	488.2	91.4	500.9	73.1	12.7	18.3
Qatar	380.0	103.2	445.8	51.5	65.7	51.7
Romania	441.7	80.0	463.6	56.4	22.0	23.7
Russian Federation	484.2	85.6	495.4	69.7	11.2	16.0
Slovak Republic	476.4	101.0	495.1	75.8	18.7	25.2
Sweden	481.5	95.7	497.1	73.8	15.5	21.9
Switzerland	523.1	92.6	529.9	81.0	6.8	11.6
Chinese Taipei	541.6	99.3	547.7	88.4	6.1	10.9
Tunisia	392.9	78.5	439.8	38.0	46.9	40.4
United Arab Emirates	441.2	91.7	468.3	62.4	27.1	29.2
United Kingdom	504.0	97.1	515.0	80.2	11.0	17.0
United States	489.4	91.9	501.1	75.7	11.7	16.2
Country mean	491.6	91.8	506.7	73.2	15.0	18.6

Notes: All countries with at least 98% enrolment rates in secondary school.

Annex E

Sample of PISA questions requiring Level 1 skills

The following sample questions from the Programme for International Student Assessment (PISA) test illustrate the skills required for 15-year-olds to perform at Level 1 proficiency. A variety of additional sample questions at different levels for the PISA assessments can be found in *PISA 2012 Results: What Students Know and Can Do (Volume I, Revised edition, February 2014): Student Performance in Mathematics, Reading and Science* (2014, OECD Publishing, Paris).

(1) Garage (Mathematics, PISA 2012)

A garage manufacturer's "basic" range includes models with just one window and one door.

George chooses the following model from the "basic" range. The position of the window and the door are shown here.

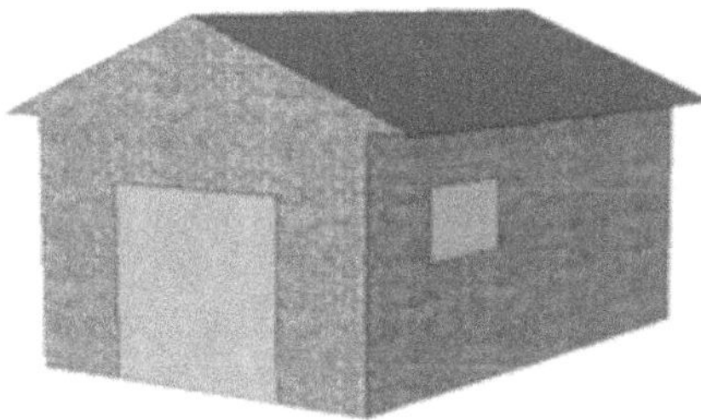

Question 1: The illustrations below show different "basic" models as viewed from the back. Only one of these illustrations matches the model above chosen by George.

Which model did George choose? Circle A, B, C or D.

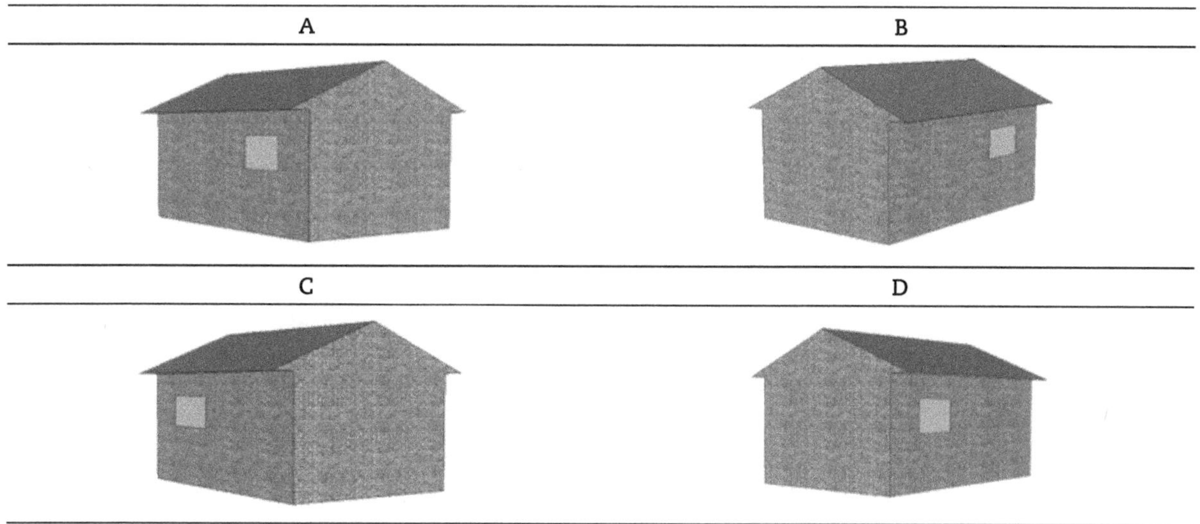

Scoring:

Question intent:

Description: Use space ability to identify a 3D view corresponding to another given 3D view

Mathematical content area: Space and shape

Context: Occupational

Process: Interpret

Full Credit: C [Graphic C]. No Credit: Other responses and missing.

Answering this question correctly corresponds to a difficulty of 420 score points on the PISA mathematics scale. Across OECD countries, 65% of students answered correctly.

Comment: Question 1 lies very close to the Level 1/Level 2 boundary on the proficiency scale. It asks students to identify a picture of a building from the back, given the view from the front. The diagrams must be interpreted in relation to the real-world positioning of "from the back", so this question is classified in the interpreting process. The correct response is C. Mental rotation tasks such as this are solved by some people using intuitive spatial visualisation. Other people need explicit reasoning processes. They may analyse the relative positions of multiple features (door, window, nearest corner), discounting the multiple choice alternatives one by one. Others might draw a bird's-eye view, and then physically rotate it. This is just one example of how different students may use quite different methods to solve PISA questions. In this case, explicit reasoning for some students is intuitive for others.

(2) Which Car? (Mathematics, PISA 2012)

Chris has just received her car driving licence and wants to buy her first car.

This table below shows the details of four cars she finds at a local car dealer.

Model:	Alpha	Bolte	Castel	Dezal
Year	2003	2000	2001	1999
Advertised price (zeds)	4800	4450	4250	3990
Distance travelled (kilometres)	105 000	115 000	128 000	109 000
Engine capacity (litres)	1.79	1.796	1.82	1.783

(In each country, the car's names were changed to other more suitable fictional names if necessary.)

Question 1: Chris wants a car that meets **all** of these conditions:

- The distance travelled is **not** higher than 120 000 kilometres.
- It was made in the year 2000 or a later year.
- The advertised price is **not** higher than 4500 zeds.

Which car meets Chris's conditions?

A. Alpha

B. Bolte

C. Castel

D. Dezal

Scoring:

Question intent:

Description: Select a value that meets four numerical conditions/statements set within a financial context

Mathematical content area: Uncertainty and data

Context: Personal

Process: Interpret

Full Credit: B Bolte. No Credit: Other responses and missing.

Answering this question correctly corresponds to a difficulty of 328 score points on the PISA mathematics scale. Across OECD countries, 81% of students answered correctly.

(3) Exchange Rate (Mathematics, PISA 2003)

Mei-Ling from Singapore was preparing to go to South Africa for 3 months as an exchange student. She needed to change some Singapore dollars (SGD) into South African rand (ZAR).

Question 1: Mei-Ling found out that the exchange rate between Singapore dollars and South African rand was:

1 SGD = 4.2 ZAR

Mei-Ling changed 3 000 Singapore dollars into South African rand at this exchange rate.

How much money in South African rand did Mei-Ling get?

Answer: ....

Scoring:

Full Credit: 12 600 ZAR (unit not required). No Credit: Other responses and missing.

Answering this question correctly corresponds to a difficulty of 406 score points on the PISA mathematics scale. Across OECD countries, 80% of students answered correctly. To answer the question correctly students have to draw on skills from the reproduction competency cluster.

(4) Speed of Racing Car (Mathematics, PISA 2000)

This graph shows how the speed of a racing car varies along a flat 3 kilometre track during its second lap.

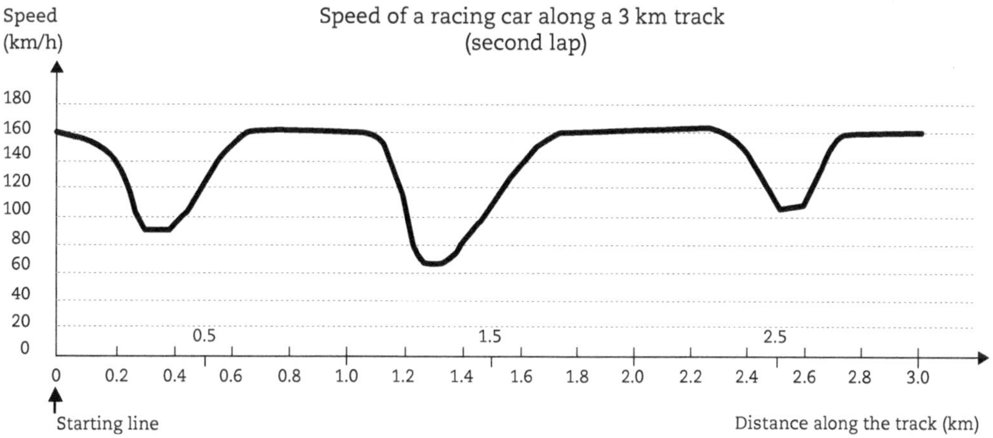

Question 2: Where was the lowest speed recorded during the second lap?

A. at the starting line.

B. at about 0.8 km.

C. at about 1.3 km.

D. halfway around the track.

Question 3: What can you say about the speed of the car between the 2.6 km and 2.8 km marks?

A. The speed of the car remains constant.

B. The speed of the car is increasing.

C. The speed of the car is decreasing.

D. The speed of the car cannot be determined from the graph.

Scoring:

Q2. Full Credit: C. at about 1.3 km. No Credit: Other responses and missing.

Answering this question correctly corresponds to a difficulty of 403 score points on the PISA mathematics scale. Across OECD countries, 84% of students answered correctly. To answer the question correctly students have to draw on skills from the reproduction competency cluster.

Q3. Full credit: B. The speed of the car is increasing. No credit: Other responses and missing.

Answering this question correctly corresponds to a difficulty of 413 score points on the PISA mathematics scale. Across OECD countries, 83% of students answered correctly. To answer the question correctly students have to draw on skills from the reproduction competency cluster.

(5) Physical Exercise (Science, PISA 2006)

Regular but moderate physical exercise is good for our health.

Question 2: What happens when muscles are exercised? Circle "Yes" or "No" for each statement.

Does this happen when muscles are exercised?	**Yes or No?**
Muscles get an increased flow of blood	Yes / No
Fats are formed in the muscles	Yes / No

Scoring:

Full Credit: Yes, No in that order. No credit: Other responses and missing.

Answering this question correctly corresponds to a difficulty of 386 score points on the PISA 2006 science scale. Across OECD countries, 82.4% of students answered correctly. This question assesses students' competency of explaining phenomena scientifically.

(6) Clothes (Science, PISA 2006)

Read the text and answer the questions that follow.

A team of British scientists is developing "intelligent" clothes that will give disabled children the power of "speech". Children wearing waistcoats made of a unique electrotextile, linked to a speech synthesizer, will be able to make themselves understood simply by tapping on the touch-sensitive material.

The material is made up of normal cloth and an ingenious mesh of carbon-impregnated fibers that can conduct electricity. When pressure is applied to the fabric, the pattern of signals that passes through the conducting fibers is altered and a computer chip can work out where the cloth has been touched. It then can trigger whatever electronic device is attached to it, which could be no bigger than two boxes of matches.

"The smart bit is in how we weave the fabric and how we send signals through it – and we can weave it into existing fabric designs so you cannot see it's in there," says one of the scientists.

Without being damaged, the material can be washed, wrapped around objects or scrunched up. The scientist also claims it can be mass-produced cheaply.

Source: Steve Farrer, "Interactive fabric promises a material gift of the garb", *The Australian*, 10 August 1998.

Question 2: Which piece of laboratory equipment would be among the equipment you would need to check that the fabric is conducting electricity?

A. Voltmeter

B. Light box

C. Micrometer

D. Sound meter

Scoring:

Full Credit: A. Voltmeter. No credit: Other responses and missing.

Answering this question correctly corresponds to a difficulty of 399 score points on the PISA 2006 science scale. Across OECD countries, 79.4% of students answered correctly.

The question only requires the student to associate electric current with a device used in electric circuits, i.e. the recall of a simple scientific fact. The competency necessary to answer this question is explaining phenomena scientifically.

(7) The Grand Canyon (Science, PISA 2006)

The Grand Canyon is located in a desert in the USA. It is a very large and deep canyon containing many layers of rock. Sometime in the past, movements in the Earth's crust lifted these layers up. The Grand Canyon is now 1.6 km deep in parts. The Colorado River runs through the bottom of the canyon.

See the picture below of the Grand Canyon taken from its south rim. Several different layers of rock can be seen in the walls of the canyon.

Question 2: There are many fossils of marine animals, such as clams, fish and corals, in the Limestone A layer of the Grand Canyon. What happened millions of years ago that explains why such fossils are found there?

A. In ancient times, people brought seafood to the area from the ocean.

B. Oceans were once much rougher and sea life washed inland on giant waves.

C. An ocean covered this area at that time and then receded later.

D. Some sea animals once lived on land before migrating to the sea.

Scoring:

Full Credit: C. No credit: Other responses and missing.

Answering this question correctly corresponds to a difficulty of 411 score points on the PISA 2006 science scale. Across OECD countries, 75.8% of students answered correctly. The question was categorised as part of the competency explaining phenomena scientifically.

ORGANISATION FOR ECONOMIC CO-OPERATION AND DEVELOPMENT

The OECD is a unique forum where governments work together to address the economic, social and environmental challenges of globalisation. The OECD is also at the forefront of efforts to understand and to help governments respond to new developments and concerns, such as corporate governance, the information economy and the challenges of an ageing population. The Organisation provides a setting where governments can compare policy experiences, seek answers to common problems, identify good practice and work to co-ordinate domestic and international policies.

The OECD member countries are: Australia, Austria, Belgium, Canada, Chile, the Czech Republic, Denmark, Estonia, Finland, France, Germany, Greece, Hungary, Iceland, Ireland, Israel, Italy, Japan, Korea, Luxembourg, Mexico, the Netherlands, New Zealand, Norway, Poland, Portugal, the Slovak Republic, Slovenia, Spain, Sweden, Switzerland, Turkey, the United Kingdom and the United States. The European Union takes part in the work of the OECD.

OECD Publishing disseminates widely the results of the Organisation's statistics gathering and research on economic, social and environmental issues, as well as the conventions, guidelines and standards agreed by its members.

OECD PUBLISHING, 2, rue André-Pascal, 75775 PARIS CEDEX 16
(91 2015 06 1P) ISBN 978-92-64-23481-9

www.ingramcontent.com/pod-product-compliance
Lightning Source LLC
LaVergne TN
LVHW081413110826
845149LV00010B/1726

* 9 7 8 9 2 6 4 2 3 4 8 1 9 *